EXPLORING JEWISH ETHICS AND VALUES

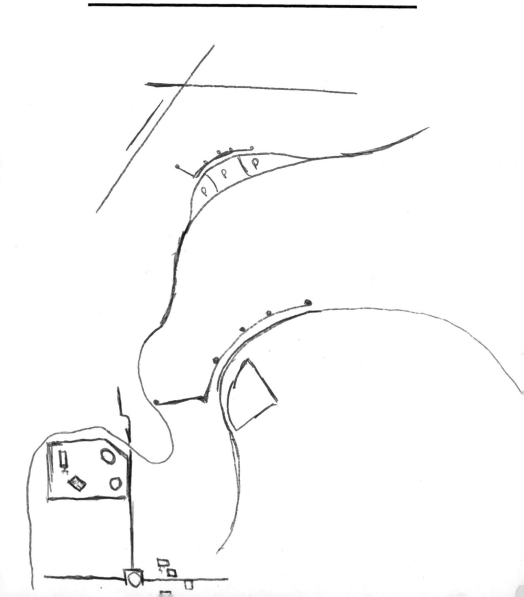

EXPLORING JEWISH ETHICS AND VALUES

by Rabbi Ronald Isaacs

KTAV Publishing House, Inc.
900 Jefferson St.
Hoboken, NJ 07030

ISBN 0-88125-652-8

KTAV Publishing House, Inc.
900 Jefferson St.
Hoboken, NJ 07030

Manufactured in United States of America

Exploring Jewish Ethics and Values

Table of Contents

INTRODUCTION

The Tanach, the Hebrew Bible, has been the source of religious ideals and wise advice for countless millions. The Talmud, reflecting the rabbinic interpretation of the Bible, conveys the noble teachings of the Bible as they relate to human life in all of its phases, secular and religious.

This book, consisting of rabbinic and biblical sayings and quotations on a variety of topics (related in the main to responsibilities to people and animals and care of the earth) is intended to provide Jewish teens with a chance to explore their own personal values. By answering the questions and discussing them in class, students have an opportunity to discover and explore their own personal values in an interesting and challenging way. Each topic is introduced with a section entitled, "What Does Judaism Have to Say." This section offers a brief introduction describing Judaism's opinion on the subject and presenting its various viewpoints. This is followed by "Quotations," consisting of statements, stories, and quotations culled from both rabbinic and biblical literature, which can be further explored in relation to the questions that follow. The quotations can be used as a personal guide for Jewish living and, it is hoped, will help to stimulate further class discussion. The final section of each chapter, simply entitled "Questions," consists of a number of engaging questions related to the topic, including hypothetical ones offering students a chance to use their imaginations to reflect and learn more about themselves and their own values. In several chapters, various exercises and role plays are also used in the Question section.

It is my hope that this book will help students develop new ways of thinking about the issues while at the same time solidifying values that they already hold dear to their hearts. In addition, I would be pleased if students began to apply Jewish principles and values they have identified into their personal decision-making. For applied Judaism not only has the power to change one's life and the world, it can also be exhilarating.

I once again want to thank all of the students in Temple Sholom's Hebrew High School and those in other communities whose commitment to Judaism and continuation of their Jewish education has served as a great source of inspiration to me and to the community at large. May they all continue to go forth from strength to strength, and may this book in some way help to change for the better the way in which they choose to live their lives.

Ronald H. Isaacs

LEADERSHIP

הַנְהָגָה

Who is the leader of all leaders?
One who can make an enemy into a friend.
(Avot de Rabbi Natan, chap. 23)

What Does Judaism Have to Say?

One way of learning about a society's values is by analyzing its leaders. Leaders should embody all the values that his or her group holds dear. Judaism has always lauded good leadership. Over the centuries there has been a wide range of advice regarding what makes for a good leader. Perhaps one of the most notable quotations on leadership is that found in *Avot de Rabbi Natan,* where the question is asked, "Who is the leader of all leaders?" The answer that is given is, "One who can make an enemy into one's friend" (*Avot de Rabbi Natan, chap. 23*).

A leader in Judaism is generally understood as one who shows us the way by going in advance, guiding and directing by virtue of wisdom, experience, or the confidence we place in him or her. A leader seems to know where we should be going and how to get us there. Good leaders also seem to have the skill to use the resources of a group, particularly the human resources, and direct them to a realization of what the members of the group hold important.

Maimonides, the great medieval philosopher identified a system of priorities in the Torah which understood that the people needed effective and committed leadership before they could secure themselves in the land and before they could establish the presence of the Temple. The king, the ancient leader in biblical times, must minimally meet four standards before he could be appointed:

1. He must ascend to the throne to fulfill a mitzvah.
2. He must be born a Jew.
3. He must be pious.
3. He must be willing to fulfill the specific mitzvot of the king.

Danny Siegel, poet and author, once wrote that among the qualities of a Jewish leader are first and foremost compassion and caring for those under his leadership. Letty Cottin Pogrebin, contributing editor of *Ms.* magazine, once wrote that a Jewish leader is someone who empowers other Jews to be more effective, humane, and secure in the larger world as well as in the Jewish community.

Henry A. Waxman, U.S. congressman from California, once wrote that a Jewish leader is any Jew whose views on matters of consequence are taken seriously by a significant number of his or her co-religionists.

Quotations on Leadership

1. In the place where there is no leader, strive to become one!

(*Talmud Berachot 6a*)

2. Ben Zoma taught: "Who is a leader? One who conquers one's passions and emotions."

3. The acts of the leader are the acts of the nation. If the leader is just, the nation is just. If the leader is unjust, the nation too is unjust and is punished for the sins of the leader.

(*Zohar ii, 47a*)

4. There are four kinds of people whom people dislike: One of them is a communal leader who is arrogant toward his constituents for no good reason.

(Talmud Pesachim 113b)

5. Who is the leader of all leaders? Some say the one who makes an enemy into one's friend.

(Talmud Avot de Rabbi Natan, ch. 23)

6. When a person is able to take abuse with a smile, that person is worthy to become a leader.

(Rabbi Nachman of Bratslav)

7. Rabbi Judah Nesiah and the rabbis disagreed. One said: "According to the leader, so goes the generation." The other said: "According to the generation, so goes the leader."

(Talmud Arachin 17a)

Questions

1. Danny Siegel, poet and author once wrote that among the qualities of a Jewish leader, the most important is being a caring and compassionate person. What is your opinion about the most important quality of good leadership? What qualities make for a great leader?

2. Who are some people who you believe are good leaders (past and present)?

3. Who in the Bible are the most prominent leaders?

4. What are some least likable qualities in leaders that you know of or leaders with whom you have actually been in contact?

5. Some Bible commentators have stated that Moses was the greatest leader of all the prophets. Do you agree? If you could have been Moses, in what ways could you have improved upon your leadership style?

6. If you could be a leader of any organization (current or in the past), what would it be and why would you want to lead it?

7. The Bible says that "in every generation a person must view himself as if he came out of Egypt." Imagine yourself having come out of Egypt as the Bible relates. Would you have voted for Moses as your leader, especially after the series of trials and tribulations the wilderness presented. Might you have supported a leader who wanted to give you more say in how things were done?

8. Can you think of situations in which you or someone else tried to lead your friends to do something they did not want to do right away? In what ways did the leader try to influence the others? Was the leader successful? What was the result of the effort?

9. Can you think of examples in your own family in which two members have tried to lead it in different directions? What were the results? Were the discussions (or perhaps arguments) focused on the different directions, or were there issues of leadership at the core?

10. *Avot de Rabbi Natan* stated that a leader is someone who can make an enemy into one's friend. Do you think this is a realistic definition of a leader? Can you think of a leader who has been able to accomplish this?

11. What are the qualities that make for good leadership on a sports team?

12. Leadership has often been thought of in Jewish tradition as an unenviable role, fraught with dangers of ambition and lust for power. Some have said that the ideal attitude is for the leader at first to express sincere unwillingness to assume the onerous position and to accept it only after much persuasion. Indeed, many famous leaders, including Moses, declared themselves unfit at the beginning of their missions. What do you believe is the ideal attitude of someone who is about to become a leader? What ought to be a leader's best and most outstanding attributes?

13. *Judah or Reuven: Who Is the Better Leader?*

Jacob was the third of our patriarchs. He was the father of thirteen children, twelve of them sons, by four different women who were his wives or concubines. His favorite wife was Rachel, and her elder son was Joseph. Jacob favored Joseph above all his other children, including those who were older. Resentment grew among the brothers, and eventually they plotted to kill their brother one day when he came out to the fields in which they worked. Here is the story in the Bible's own words. Read the story and decide who displayed the stronger leadership—Judah or Reuven.

And the brothers said to one another, "Look, this dreamer is coming. Now let us kill him and throw him into one of the pits, and we will say, 'An evil beast has eaten him.' We will see what becomes of his dreams." And Reuven heard it and rescued him from them and said, "Let us not take his life." And Reuven said to them, "Shed no blood. Throw him into this pit in the wilderness, but do not lay a hand on him." He meant to rescue him from their hands and return him to his father. So when Joseph came to his brothers, they stripped Joseph of his coat of many colors which he was wearing, and they took him and threw him into the pit, an empty pit with no water. They sat down to eat bread and looked up and saw a band of Ishmaelites coming from Gil'ad, with their camels bearing spices, balm, and jewels, on their way down to Egypt. And Judah said to his brother, "What is the profit in killing our brother and hiding his blood? Come, let us sell him to the Ishmaelites and let our hand not be upon him, for he is our brother, our flesh." And his brothers listened to him.

(Genesis 37:19–27)

The rabbis also reviewed this story in terms of the actions of Reuven and Judah, and they made some interesting comments. After reading their comments, decide who the better choice for leader was according to rabbinic thought.

a. Judah's protest was part of the evidence that the Israelites observed the Ten Commandments even before the Torah was given, because Judah knew that we were not to commit murder (Midrash).

b. Nachmonides: Reuven persuaded the brothers not to commit murder, but Judah convinced them that they would be just as guilty of murder by neglect as they would be by action.

c. The sages: Judah's actions did not go far enough. Drawing their conclusion from the fact that the biblical text states, "and his brothers listened to him," the sages held that the brothers would have listened had Judah said to rescue Joseph as well (i.e., Judah started the process of redemption but did not complete it).

FRIENDSHIP

יְדִידוּת

Let the honor of your friend be
as dear to you as your own.
(*Pirke Avot 2:15*)

What Does Judaism Have to Say?

People often say that they have many acquaintances,
but there are few people who admit to having more than
one or two really good friends. The Hebrew word *chaver* is
often used in rabbinical writings to mean friend or
companion.

Friendship is a very important value in Judaism.
One of the seven wedding blessings petitions God to grant
joy to these loving companions. Here we see that according
to the rabbis, husband and wife were considered to be
friends.

The model friendship of Jonathan and David some
3,000 years ago (as portrayed in the Book of Samuel I) is
held in high esteem. What makes their friendship
especially remarkable is that these two men had
competitive interests. Jonathan was the oldest son of King
Saul and heir apparent to the throne. David, King Saul's
leading soldier, was the people's choice to be the future
king. Yet their potential competition never stood in the way
of their friendship. David's greater gift of leadership only
increased Jonathan's desire to be the top aide in his
friend's future kingdom: "You are going to be king over
Israel and I shall be second to you" (*I Samuel 23:17*)

Since friendships such as that of David and Jonathan are rather unusual these days, Judaism urges that one be very careful when choosing his or her friends.

Quotations on Friendship

1. Let the honor of your friend be as dear to you as your own.

(Pirke Avot 2:15)

2. On the day of your friend's success, participate in his joy.

(Ecclesiastes Rabbah 7)

3. Do not make friends with a person who is given to anger.

(Proverbs 22:24)

4. Never judge your friend until you put yourself in his position.

(Pirke Avot 2:5)

5. To pull a friend out of the mire, do not hesitate to get dirty.

(Baal Shem Tov)

6. When you make a friend, begin by testing him, and be in no hurry to trust him.

(Wisdom of Ben Sira 6:7)

7. One who elevates himself at the expense of his friend's shame has no share in the World to Come.

(Jerusalem Talmud Chagigah 2,1)

8. He who harps on a matter alienates a friend.

(Proverbs 17:9)

9. If you want to lose a friend, lend him money.

(Common Proverb)

10. Your good conduct will make you friends, but your evil conduct will make you enemies.

(Mishnah Eduyot 5:7)

Questions

1. Who is your best friend? What are the qualities that you most admire in this person?

2. What are the advantages of having good friends?

3. Do you think you could have a true friendship with someone who was not of the Jewish faith? Why or why not? Are there advantages to having friends who are Jewish?

4. What must you do to keep a friendship strong? Why do you believe that some friendships dissolve while others are long-lasting?

5. Is it possible to have a good friend who is much older or younger than you? Do you have such a friend?

6. Do you believe that friends ought to be sharing secrets with one another?

7. If you and your best friend were running in a competition for class president, do you think that you could pursue this goal and still remain best friends?

8. How do you go about criticizing a friend when criticism is due?

9. Following are the traits that studies have shown to be highly desirable in attracting people to become friends. Share with a partner in your class your feelings toward each of these traits. Then talk to your partner about other character traits that you find attractive in any person who is likely to become your friend:

> Pleasantness
> Standing up for one's convictions
> Considerateness
> Reliability
> Sense of humor
> Ability to carry on a conversation

10. *The Story of Two Close Friends*

Read the following story and have a class discussion on the value of friendship as displayed in this story. Choose a partner and discuss with him or her the value of having a good friend. As part of your deliberations, make a list of the advantages of having a friend and the ways in which your life would be different if you did not have any close friends.

There were two close friends who had been parted by war so that they lived in different kingdoms. Once one of them came to visit his friend, and because he came from the city of the king's enemy, he was imprisoned and sentenced to be executed as a spy. No amount of pleas would save him, so he begged the king for one kindness.

"Your majesty," he said, "let me have just one month to return to my land and put my affairs in order so my family will be cared for after my death. At the end of the month I will return to pay the penalty."

"How can I believe you will return?" answered the king. "What security can you offer?"

"My friend will be my security," said the man. "He will pay for my life with his if I do not return."

The king called in the man's friend, and to his amazement, the friend agreed to the conditions.

On the last day of the month, the sun was setting, and the man had not yet returned. The king ordered his friend killed in his stead. As the sword was about to descend, the man returned and quickly placed the sword on his own neck. But his friend stopped him.

"Let me die for you," he pleaded.

The king was deeply moved. He ordered the sword to be taken away and pardoned both of them.

"Since there is such great love and friendship between the two of you," he said, "I entreat you to let me join you as a third."

And from that day on they became the king's companions. And it was in this spirit that our sages of blessed memory said, "Get yourself a companion." (Legend in *Beit HaMidrash,* Adolf Jellinek)

11. From the writings of the *Menorat ha-Maor,* a biblical commentary, we learn what advice he gives to a person who wants to show that he or she is truly a friend:

Be first to greet your fellow man; invite him to your joyful occasions; call him by complimentary names; never give away his secrets; help him when he is in trouble; look after his interests when he is away; overlook his shortcomings and forgive him promptly; criticize him when he has done wrong; respect him always; do not deceive him; do not lie to him; pray for him and wish him happiness; attend to his burial if he dies.

What is the advice that you would give to someone who wants to show that he or she is truly worthy of being a friend of another? List your top ten choices of advice for friendship:

1. _____
2. _____
3. _____
4. _____
5. _____
6. _____
7. _____
8. _____
9. _____
10. _____

HOSPITALITY

הַכְנָסַת אוֹרְחִים

Let all who are hungry come and eat.
(Passover Haggadah)

What Does Judaism Have to Say?

In Jewish law, hospitality (*hachnasat orchim*) is not just a pleasant social nicety but a serious legal obligation. Inhospitality, on the other hand, is viewed not only as ungracious behavior but as vile and forbidden.

Abraham, Judaism's first patriarch, is extolled by the rabbis for his virtue of hospitality. Whenever presented with an opportunity to serve guests, he does so with swiftness and courtesy: "When he (Abraham) raised his eyes he saw three men standing at a distance from him. As soon as he saw them, he ran from the entrance of the tent door to greet them (*Genesis 18:2*)."

In rabbinic thought, sharing one's table is preferred to giving money to the poor and the needy. The first is a personal act, while the second is a more impersonal one. Jewish law insists that a host be hospitable and generous, and it demands that a guest be grateful as well. Even in the Blessing after the Meal, the *Birkat HaMazon*, the guest traditionally inserts a special blessing on behalf of his host's family.

One of the few instances in Jewish law when a person is allowed to fib is when asked if he or she enjoyed being a guest at somebody's house. The guest should reply yes, whether or not that is so. If one did enjoy his or her experience, one should say so, but should hold back from total and complete praise, lest the gracious host be overwhelmed by unwanted guests!

In legendary Jewish literature, Job is represented as a man of hospitality. We are told that he built an inn at the crossroads with four doors opening in four directions, so that transients might have no trouble finding an entrance.

As with other mitzvot that were concretized into institutions, many Jewish communities established and maintained hospitality societies to help visitors find comfort and hospitality in a strange environment.

Even today, the commandment of hospitality is one of the most pleasant to perform. Any Jew who travels extensively and has made contact with Jews in other lands can testify how pleasant it is to enjoy Jewish hospitality when away from home.

Quotations on Hospitality

A. Responsibilities of the Host

1. Let your house be open wide; treat the poor as members of your own family.

(Pirke Avot 1:4)

2. In Jerusalem there was a custom of displaying a flag in front of the door, thereby indicating that the meal was ready and that guests might come in and eat. The removal of the flag was a sign that the meal was finished and that guests should cease from entering.

(Talmud Baba Batra 93b)

3. It is the duty of the host to be cheerful during meals and thus make his guests feel at home and comfortable at the table.

(Derech Eretz Zuta 9)

4. It is unbecoming for a host to eat before his guest.

(*Derech Eretz Zuta, 8*)

5. A person should not enter a house suddenly, without ringing or knocking.

(*Derech Eretz Rabbah 5, 2*)

6. Always be happy when you are sitting at your table and those who are hungry are enjoying your hospitality.

(*Talmud Derech Eretz Zuta 9*)

7. Never embarrass your guests by staring at them.

(*Mishneh Torah, Laws of Blessings 7:6*)

8. Guests should not overstay their welcome.

(*Talmud Pesachim 49a*)

B. Responsibilities of a Guest

1. Our rabbis taught: Every scholar who feasts much in every place eventually destroys his home, widows his wife, orphans his young, forgets his learning and becomes involved in many quarrels.

(*Talmud Pesachim 49a*)

2. Ben Zoma used to say, "What does a good guest say?"

"'How much trouble my host goes through for me. How much meat he has offered. How much wine he has set before me. How many cakes he has brought before me. And all this trouble he went through for me.'"

"But an inconsiderate guest, what does he say?"

"'What trouble has my host gone through? I have eaten one piece of bread and a single piece of meat. I have had but one cup of wine. All the trouble the host has gone to has been only for his family.'"

(*Talmud Berachot 58a*)

3. A guest should comply with every request that the host makes of him.

(*Derech Eretz Rabbah 6*)

4. It is unbecoming for a guest to bring another guest. More unbecoming is the guest who puts his host to great trouble.

(Derech Eretz Zuta 8)

5. A guest should not enter a house suddenly, without ringing or knocking.

(Derech Eretz Rabbah 5, 2)

6. A guest should not drink his goblet in one gulp. This is unmannerly.

(Talmud Betzah 25b)

7. If you are a guest in a certain place, conduct yourself in conformity with local custom.

(Zohar I, 144a)

8. A guest should not say to the host, "Serve me that I may eat," but must wait until he is invited to eat.

(Derech Eretz Rabbah 57a)

Questions

1. What are some ways in which you try to make an invited guest feel welcome and comfortable?

2. Have you ever been invited as a guest to someone's home and not felt comfortable? Why? What could have been done for you to make you feel more at ease?

3. What kinds of guests do you most enjoy having at your house? Why?

4. If you eat a meal in another's home and find it totally unappetizing, do you:
   a. praise the host/hostess for it
   b. say nothing
   c. tell the truth.

5. Who do you believe benefits more from hospitality, the guest or the host? Who do you feel ought to benefit the most?

6. A guest has just finished spending a day at the home of his host. Can you think of some nice things that a guest could do for his host after returning home? What might a good host do for the guest?

7. If you could improve yourself to become a better guest, what would the improvements be?

8. Exercise: Divide into pairs, with one person being the guest and the other being the host. Have the guest and the host take turns reading the quotations in the "Quotations" section related to the ethics of being a guest and a host. Think about real-life situations to which the statements relate and whether you feel that the advice given is sound advice in today's world.

9. As an example of communities' responding to the challenge of integrating new families into the community, groups called Welcome Wagons were formed. If you were the head of a Welcome Wagon group, what would be some goals that you would like to accomplish?

BUSINESS ETHICS

מוּסָר

You shall not oppress a hired servant
who is poor and needy.
(*Deuteronomy 24:14*)

What Does Judaism Have to Say?

Jewish texts and teachings are filled with examples of concern with earning a living but doing so in an ethical and moral manner. Interestingly, more than a hundred commandments in the Torah address the themes of business and economics. Biblical laws were concerned with a worker's welfare and dignity.

During the decade of the 1980s, applications to business schools rose significantly. However, by the end of the decade, insider trading scandals brought the downfall of many leading business entrepreneurs. Several kosher butcher shops were cited, fined, and closed for selling non-kosher meat, and a large Passover matzah manufacturer was fined for conspiring with competitors to fix prices. These and other incidents have led to questions such as these: Are businesses intrinsically unethical? Are big businesses getting out of hand?

Centuries ago the prophets were often seen preaching from the marketplace, not from a lectern in the Temple in Jerusalem. They denounced employers who did not pay their workers on time. The Prophet Jeremiah, for instance, castigated employers who "build their houses with unfairness and who make their fellow human being work without pay" (*22:13*). The Prophet Amos denounced the economic sins of the upper class, such as allowing financial gain to override justice (*2:6*).

Many of the prophetic teachings regarding justice and righteousness in these areas were given concrete expression by rabbinic thinkers. The ancient rabbis reminded us that the first question that we human beings will be asked upon reaching the World to Come is whether or not we were honest in our business dealings (*Talmud Shabbat 31a*). Talmudic literature is filled with laws governing commercial life, such as how an employer is to behave toward his employees and the duties of employees to their employer. Topics include:

1. Which prices are legitimate and which constitute overcharging
2. How false weights and measures are to be avoided
3. How conditions of a sale are binding
4. What is fair and unfair competition
5. How a worker is to be paid

The principles developed to govern business relations, labor, and management are still very much applicable today. It would be wonderful if all people would heed the timeless wisdom of the Talmud, which stated, "Whoever wants to be saintly should live according to the tractates of the Talmud dealing with commerce and finance" (*Talmud Baba Kamma 30a*).

Quotations on Business Ethics

A. Duty to Work

In Judaism, it is a person's duty to work, and Judaism has always stressed the importance of the work ethic and being a productive worker. A person who works is enabled to be self-supporting. The Ten Commandments (*Exodus 20:9*) command a person to work six days a week, but to rest on the seventh day. Adam is told to work and till the soil.

Perhaps the most notable quotation on the duty to work and have a trade is the following, which appears in the Talmudic tractate of *Kiddushin 29a:*

"In addition to teaching his child Torah, a father must also teach him a trade and how to swim."

B. Obligations of the Worker

1. There is a general tendency for a worker to labor faithfully for his employer throughout a period of two or three hours, and then to become lazy at his job.

(Midrash, Genesis Rabbah 70:18)

2. A worker is not permitted to labor at night and to hire himself out during the day, to plow with his cow in the evenings and hire her out in the mornings, nor should he go hungry and afflict himself in order to feed his children—for this is tantamount to stealing from the labor of the employer.

(Tosefta, Talmud Baba Metzia, chap. 8)

3. Fifty productive men are better than two hundred who are not.

(Jerusalem Talmud Peah 8:8)

4. A person should love work and not hate work. For just as the Torah was given as a covenant, so work was given as a covenant, as it is said: "Six days you shall labor to do all of your work, but the seventh day is a Sabbath to God [Exodus 20:9–10]."

(Avot de Rabbi Natan, chap. 11)

5. Splendid is the study of Torah when combined with some worldly occupation, for toil in them both puts sin out of the mind.

(Pirke Avot 2:2)

6. A worker must be very punctual in the matter of time.

(Maimonides, *Mishneh Torah, Laws of Hiring, chap. 13)*

C. Obligation of the Employer

Jewish tradition lays the foundation for protecting the rights of workers, extending those rights to poor persons who often had to sell themselves as servants in order to survive. Shaped by biblical concepts, talmudic rulings insisted on scrupulous fairness toward all workers. To the extent possible, the sages always gave an employee the benefit of the doubt in a dispute with an employer.

1. It is obligatory for an employer to set aside time for the workers to eat and say the Grace after Meals and prayers.
(Code of Jewish Law, Orach Chayim, 100:191)

2. You shall not oppress a hired servant who is poor and needy. In the same day you shall give him his wages.
(Deuteronomy 24:14-15)

3. A person's drive for profit should be prompted by the desire to give *tzedakah.*
(Rabbi Nachman of Bratslav)

4. Whoever withholds an employee's wages, it is as though he has taken the person's life from him.
(Talmud Baba Metzia 112a)

5. When you reap the harvest of your land, you shall not reap all the edges of your field, or gather the gleanings of your harvest. You shall leave them for the poor and the stranger, for I am God.
(Leviticus 19:10)

D. Obligations of the Consumer

Business consumers also have obligations in connection with their purchases. They are expected to show courtesy and consideration to both the business owner and the consumers. Here are some quotations from Jewish tradition:

1. Just as fraud applies to buying and selling, it can also apply to spoken words. A person should not say, "How much does this object cost?" if he has no intention of buying it.

(*Talmud Baba Metzia 4:4*)

2. A person should not pretend to be interested in making a purchase when he has no money.

(*Talmud Baba Metzia, 58b*)

Questions

1. Why do you believe that the Torah wanted workers to be paid on the same day? Can you think of any modern examples of a kind of worker that would need to be paid on the same day that he or she did a job?

2. Do you know of any modern examples where a worker receives the fringe benefit of being fed by his or her employer?

3. A kosher dairy restaurant has been in business for ten years in a certain town. A business entrepreneur has gone to that town's zoning board for permission to open a similar kosher dairy restaurant directly across the street from the first one. If you were on the town's zoning board, would you grant permission to the entrepreneur? Upon which principles of business ethics would you base your decision?

4. At a recent Jewish educational conference Vendor A was marketing Israeli kipot and doing a brisk business. In another shop a few feet away, Vendor B was selling similar kipot, but at a higher price. Vendor B was upset that Vendor A was selling the kipot for less than his own selling price. He went to the management of the educational conference, arguing that his competitor's shop ought to be charging the same price as his shop. He also mentioned that if he had to sell his kipot for the same price as that of

Vendor A, he would be selling them at his cost and not making any money at all. Do you feel that Vendor B has just cause to be upset? Why or why not? If you were part of the educational conference's management, how would you decide this case?

5. Have you even been faced with a tough ethical decision related to the workplace? How did you deal with it?

6. What are some things that employers could be doing to make Jewish ethical teachings come more alive?

7. The Torah teaches us that in an agricultural society one was commanded to leave the corners of the field uncut so that the poor could help themselves to what was left behind. In addition, a reaper was to let grain stalks fall to the ground so that the poor could find them. How could a businessperson today apply these two commandments to his or her work?

8. Do you think advertising companies that create ads for cigarette companies are acting ethically, knowing that what they are promoting is injurious to one's health? Would this be a case of "profiting by the blood of your neighbor"?

9. Rabbi Joshua Heschel, noted theologian, was reported as saying the following in one of his classes on business ethics: "When there is blood in an egg, it is rendered unkosher and is not allowed to be eaten. My dear students, I hope that you will be just as capable of spotting blood in money as well." What do you think Heschel meant by this statement?

10. What are some nice ways in which you have seen a business showing its appreciation to customers?

11. In an article in the late 1960s in the *Harvard Business Review*, the author suggested that people who do not engage in deception in the workplace will never accumulate money or power. What is your reaction to this statement? How would the rabbis react to this?

12. Why do you think the rabbis wrote that customers who had no money or were not interested in a purchase should not pretend to be interested? Have you ever spent time with a salesperson knowing that you were not interested or prepared to make a purchase that day? Can you think of, an occasion when spending time with a salesperson about a particular item (even though you have no intent to buy) is justifiable?

13. In recent years, American companies have begun to adopt as part of their mission statement a code of ethics, which outlines responsibilities of employer to employees and company to the consumer. Imagine you are the president of a large company. Below, develop a code of ethics. You may choose to work with a classmate.

1. _____
2. _____
3. _____
4.._____
5. _____

EDUCATION

חִנּוּךְ

He who teaches a child
is like one who creates him.
(Talmud Sanhedrin 19a)

What Does Judaism Have to Say?

Emphasis on the importance of education in Jewish tradition dates back to biblical times. The Israelites were constantly being commanded to study all of the laws and commandments that they were taught. God's first charge to Joshua, successor to Moses, was "Let not this book of teaching cease from your lips, but recite it day and night, that you may observe faithfully all that is in it (*Joshua 1:8*)."

By talmudic times, learning and study had come to be regarded as so important that scholars stood out as the elite of Jewish society, exercising authority in many community activities. Scholars, rather than businessmen, held authority over community activities. Teachers, by and large, received no fees. The reason was that the rabbis classified teaching not as an occupation but as a holy and noble duty. Some sages had such a lofty conception of the importance of the teacher that they envisioned God Himself as a teacher: "What then does God do in the fourth quarter? God sits and instructs the schoolchildren," they recorded in the Talmud (*Avodah Zarah 3b*). The teacher–student relationship has always been considered a sacred one, and there are numerous statements dealing with this most important relationship.

Quotations on Education

A. Students

A Jewish student's first visit to a classroom and the first lesson the student received were traditionally enveloped with much emotion and ceremony. When the young child entered the classroom on opening day, he or she received a clean slate onto which letters of the Hebrew alphabet or a simple biblical verse had been written in honey. The child licked off the slate while reciting the name of each Hebrew letter, and afterward ate treats of honey cake and apples.

By the time of the Talmud, study was already placed at such a high premium that scholarly students stood out among the elite, often holding authority over community organizations.

Following are quotations related to the student:

1. The world endures only for the sake of the breath of schoolchildren.

(Talmud Shabbat 119b)

2. A person should always live in the same town as his teacher.

(Talmud Berachot 8a)

3. The student who pays respect to his teacher, it is as if he were paying respect to the Divine Presence.

(Jerusalem Talmud, Eruvin 5:1)

4. A student is required to carry a torch and walk in front of his teacher. A student is required to help his teacher dress, put on shoes, and is also required to stand by his teacher while he sleeps.

(Yalkut Shimoni, Beshallach 226)

5. Whoever contends against the ruling of a teacher, it is as though he contended with the Divine Presence. Whoever expresses resentment against his teacher, it is as though he expressed it against the Divine Presence.

(*Talmud Sanhedrin 110a*)

6. The Torah says, "And you shall honor." This means one shall not stand in his teacher's regular place, nor sit in his regular place, nor contradict his statements. When one asks him a law, one must do so with reverence. One must not be quick in replying to him, nor interrupt his words.

(*Numbers Rabbah 15:17*)

7. When one piece of iron sharpens another, so do two students sharpen each other [when they study together].

(*Ta'anit 7a*)

Questions on Students

1. From the rabbinic texts, what do you see as the differences between a student-teacher relationship in ancient times and one today? Which, in your opinion, is preferable?

2. Do you feel that teachers today are receiving the respect that rabbinic opinion seems to favor? Describe the kind of teacher that most commands your respect.

3. A rabbinic opinion was expressed that it was improper to argue with a teacher's ruling and that one who did so was contending with the Divine Presence. Why do you think this ruling was made? Do you agree with it? Are there times when you need to contend with a teacher's ruling?

B. Teachers

1. No teacher should be appointed for the young unless he is a God-fearing person and possesses the qualifications to teach accurately.

(*Code of Jewish Law, Yoreh Deah 245:17*)

2. The easily angered person cannot teach.

(*Pirke Avot 2:5*)

3. *Talmudic Story*

Rabbi Perioda had a student with whom he found it
necessary to rehearse a lesson many times before the latter
comprehended it. One day the rabbi was hurriedly called
away to perform a charitable act. Before he departed,
however, he repeated the lesson at hand the usual number
of times, but, on this occasion, his pupil failed to learn it.

"Why is it, my son," asked Rabbi Perioda, "that the
repetitions this time have been thrown away?"

The student replied, "Because, Master, my mind was
so preoccupied with the summons you received to
discharge another duty."

"Well, then," said the rabbi, "Let us begin again."

And he repeated the lesson again the usual number
of times. [Rabbi Perioda was rewarded with a long life.]

(Talmud Eruvin 54b)

4. [The Ark was] overlaid with gold from within and from
without; so too the teacher's inner and outer self should be
consistent.

(Talmud Yoma 72b)

5. If a teacher is incompetent, his words seem to the
students as harsh as falling rain. If the teacher is
competent, his teaching is distilled gently like dew.

(Talmud Ta'anit 7a)

6. He who teaches a child is as if he had created it.

(Talmud Sanhedrin 19a)

7. God said: You must teach, as I taught, without a fee.

(Talmud Nedarim 37a)

Questions on Teachers

1. Have you ever had a teacher who was very interested in
your activities aside from school work? How did it feel to
have such a teacher? Did you find that such a teacher had

more of an influence upon you than others who took less interest in your personal life?

2. What are your criteria for a good teacher? How do they compare to some of the rabbinic advice that you have just read?

3. Who are some of the best teachers you have ever had? Why do you feel this way about him or her?

4. Many rabbinical students have reported opportunities of visiting with their teachers in their homes. Have you ever been invited to the home of your teacher? If yes, what were your experiences? If not, would you like to be invited?

5. Describe the difference between relationships you have had with your rabbi and Hebrew school teachers versus those with the teachers in your secular school. Which relationships were the stronger of the two? Why?

6. Are there any teachers that you call by their first name? Do you feel that doing this is respectful?

7. What did the rabbis mean by their statement, "He who teaches a child is as if he had created it"?

C. Educational Methods

A student may bring out the best in a teacher just as a teacher may bring out the best in a student. Each owes the other respect and loyalty. The rabbis, in considering a teacher the most exalted person in a student's life, had many ideas about teaching techniques. Following are quotations from Jewish tradition related to educational methods.

1. Rabbah would first put his students into a joyous, cheerful mood before starting on the lesson.

(Talmud Pesachim 117a)

2. Rabbah said, "One should always study that part of the Torah to which the student's interest draws him."

(Talmud Avodah Zarah 19a)

3. If a student is inattentive, put that student next to a diligent student.

(*Talmud Baba Batra 21a*)

4. A teacher must not become angry with his students if they do not understand him, but must repeat his explanation as many times as necessary until they do understand.

(*Code of Jewish Law, Yoreh Deah 246:10*)

5. The honor of a student should be as dear to you as your own.

(*Pirke Avot 4:12*)

6. Rabi was once lecturing when he noticed that his audience was falling asleep. Searching for ways to arouse them, he suddenly called out, "A woman in Egypt gave birth to six hundred thousand children all at once."

One student, Rabbi Ishmael ben Yose, stirred out of his boredom, asked, "Who could that be?"

Rabi said loudly, "It was Yocheved when she gave birth to Moses, because he is equal to six hundred thousand people."

(*Song of Songs Rabbah 1:65*)

Questions: Role Playing

Here are two situations for you to role-play with your classmates:

1. Choose a partner and have one play the role of teacher and the other the student's role. Tell each other what you most enjoy and appreciate about the other. Then tell each other some things about each other that you would like to see improved to enhance the educational experience in the classroom. Change roles and repeat the exercise.

2. You are a member of a panel of judges that is expected to choose a "Teacher of the Year" from a list of candidates. Choose a partner (who is also a judge on the panel) and discuss your ideal teacher of the year based on the quotations sources in this chapter.

FAMILY HARMONY

שָׁלוֹם בַּיִת

To honor parents is more important
even than to honor God.
(Jerusalem Talmud Peah 1:1)

What Does Judaism Have to Say?

The Jewish people have been called the People of the Book, but we are surely the people of the family. We began centuries ago as one family with Abraham, Isaac, and Jacob, and we have grown tremendously over the centuries. Through the many difficult times during our history, strong family ties have always been an important strategy for Jewish survival.

Jewish biblical and rabbinic tradition has many statements and advice on building a strong family and home. Many comments relate to obligations that children have toward their parents. One of the most famous is the one in the Ten Commandments: Honor your father and your mother (Exodus 20:12). The Book of Leviticus 19:3 states, "A person should revere his [or her] mother and father." As can be expected, the rabbis often debated the true meaning of "honor" and "revere," and they detailed examples of what it meant to honor and revere one's parents.

Much of the advice presented in rabbinic and biblical literature centuries ago is still very much applicable and, if heeded, would undoubtedly strengthen the bonds between parents and their children.

Quotations on Family Harmony

A. Family and Home

Growing up today is much more complicated than it was a generation or two ago. Today there are often tensions from outside forces that were less prevalent when your parents were growing up. For example, with more leisure time today, there are more organizations competing for the attention of your family, which potentially could reduce the time spent with your parents. In many families both parents are part of the work force, further decreasing contact time between parents and their children.

Following are biblical and rabbinic quotations related to the family and the home.

1. A home where Torah is not heard will not endure.

(Introd. Tikkune Zohar 6a)

2. Anger in a home is like a worm in a fruit.

(Talmud Sotah 3b)

3. A man should honor his wife and children with even more than he can afford.

(Talmud Chullin 84b)

4. Happy is the man who fears God and who is ardently devoted to God's commandments. Wealth and riches are in his house, and his beneficence lasts forever.

(Psalm 112:1,3)

5. He who loves his wife as himself, who honors her more than himself, who rears his children in the right path, and who marries them off at the proper time, concerning him it is written: "And you shall know that your home is at peace" [Job 5:24].

(Talmud Yevamot 62b)

B. Children's Obligations to Their Parents

What are some ways in which you honor your parents? In what ways would you like to have your own children honor you? The mitzvah of honoring one's parents is one of the few religious obligations in the Torah with promise of a reward attached to it. Placing it in the Torah in this way stresses its importance: "Honor your mother and your father, so that your days may be long on the land that God gives you" (*Deuteronomy 5:16*). According to the Mishnah, honoring parents is one of the mitzvot for which one is rewarded both in this world and in the world to come (*Talmud Peah 1:1*).

In order to help us better understand what "honoring one's parents" means in everyday life, the rabbis have taught that honoring them includes providing them with food, drink, and clothing, as well as guiding their footsteps as they grow older.

Leviticus 19:3 states that "a person should revere his mother and father." The rabbis debated the meaning of this text. Some said that it means literally to stand in awe of them, while others suggested that it means we should respect them because we are afraid of them. According to another interpretation, in the Talmud (*Kiddushin 31b*), to revere one's parents means that a child should not sit in their chair, speak in their place, or contradict what they say.

Following are some quotations related to children's obligations to their parents:

1. There are three partners in humankind: The Holy Blessed One, the father and the mother. When a person honors his father, and his mother, God says, "It is as though I had dwelt among them and they had honored Me."

(*Talmud Kiddushin 30b*)

2. "Honor your father and your mother." I might have understood that because the word "father" precedes in the

text, he should actually take precedence over the mother. But in another passage it states, "You shall each revere his mother and his father" [*Leviticus 19:3*], the mother preceding. Scripture thus declares that both are equal.

(*Mechilta of Rabbi Ishmael, "Pisha," chap. 1*)

3. To honor parents is more important even than to honor God.

(*Jerusalem Talmud, Peah 1:1*)

4. Whether you have wealth or not, honor your parents.

(*Jerusalem Talmud, Peah 1:1*)

5. If a parent unwittingly transgresses a law of the Torah, his child shall not reprimand him, "Father, you have violated a law."

Rather, he should say, "Father, is that what it says in the Torah?"

But in the end, aren't both expressions equally insulting?

Yes. What he should really say is, "Father, the Torah says such-and-such."

(*Talmud Sanhedrin 81a*)

A. Story About Honoring a Mother

6. Rabbi Tarfon's mother once walked in the courtyard on the Sabbath and her sandal split and fell off. Rabbi Tarfon placed his two hands under her feet so that she walked on them until she reached her bed.

One time Rabbi Tarfon became ill, and the sages came to visit him. His mother said to them, "Pray for Rabbi Tarfon, my sons, for he honors me more than he should."

They asked him what he did for her and she told them what had happened. They said to her, "Even if he were to do that a thousand times, he would not have given you even half the honor demanded by the Torah."

(*Jerusalem Talmud, Kiddushin 1:7*)

7. To what length should the duty of honoring parents go? Even were they to take a purse of his, full of gold, and cast it in his presence into the sea, he must not shame them, manifest grief in their presence, or display any anger, but accept the Divine decree without demurral.

(Mishneh Torah, Book of Judges, Mamrim, chap. 6:7)

8. One should not call his father by his first name, neither during nor after his lifetime, except to identify him to others.

(Code of Jewish Law, Yoreh Deah, chap. 240)

9. It was asked of Rabbi Ulla: "How far must a child go in respecting his parents?" Rabbi Ulla replied: "Consider what a certain pagan named Dama, the son of Nathina, did in the city of Ashkelon. The sages once desired merchandise from him for which he would make a 600,000 gold dinarim profit. But the key to the room in which the merchandise was kept was lying under Dama's sleeping father. Dama would not trouble his father in order to complete the transaction."

(Talmud Kiddushin 31b)

Questions on Children's Obligations to Their Parents

1. In what ways are honoring parents similar to honoring God?

2. The commandment to honor one's parents has a built-in reward, namely length of days. In what way do you think that honoring a parent can lead to longevity of years for a child?

3. What in your opinion is the difference between "being in awe of" a parent and "honoring" a parent?

4. The Bible commands a child to honor and revere his parents, but there is no command related to loving one's parents. Why do you think the Bible does not make "loving one's parents" a mitzvah?

5. Imagine that one of your parents is a heavy smoker. You know that smoking has been shown to be bad for one's health. Do you feel that you are obliged to try to convince your parent to stop smoking?

C. Parents' Obligations to Their Children

The Jewish people was first and foremost a family. Abraham, Isaac, Jacob, Sarah, Rebekah, Rachel, and Leah are still referred to today as our Jewish patriarchs and matriarchs rather than our founders or leaders. And the Jewish people are still called the Children of Israel.

Perhaps the most famous statement about a parent's obligations to children appears in the Talmud, which gives a list of those things a parent is obliged to provide for a child:

A father is obligated to do the following for his son: circumcise him, redeem him if he is a firstborn, teach him Torah, teach him to swim, find him a wife, and teach him a trade.

(Talmud Kiddushin 29a)

Many now interpret this passage to mean that both parents—mother and father—are obligated to do these things for their child. From this statement we can see that rabbinic tradition was concerned not only with intellectual and spiritual competency of children, but also with knowledge of practical skills and survival. Once again, the commandment to love a child was not highlighted in rabbinic tradition. Perhaps the rabbis believed that this was an area unlikely to be neglected.

Following are quotations related to parents' obligations toward their children:

1. You shall diligently teach them to your children.
(Deuteronomy 6:7)

2. The rabbis say that the best skill a parent can teach his child is the study of Torah, for it will provide for him in this world and sustain him in the World to Come.
(Talmud Kiddushin 82a)

3. A parent who does not rebuke his children leads him into delinquency.
(Exodus Rabbah 1:1)

4. Rabbah said that a parent should never show favoritism among his children.
(Talmud Shabbat 10b)

5. Rabbi Judah says: Anyone who does not teach his child a craft may be regarded as if he is teaching him to steal.
(Talmud Kiddushin 29a)

6. The education of young girls is entrusted to the mother and she must educate them in the proper manner to sew and to cook. Also she shall teach them the quality of modesty.
(Otzar Dinim U'minhagim 139)

7. A person should not promise to give a child something and then not give it, because in that way the child learns to lie.
(Talmud Sukkah 46b)

8. A father once came to the Baal Shem Tov with a problem concerning his son. He complained that the son was forsaking Judaism and morality and asked the rabbi what he could do. The Baal Shem Tov answered: "Love him more."
(Chasidic Tale)

Questions on Parents' Obligations to Their Children

1. Dr. Jerome Bruner, an educational psychologist, once said, "I think parents should forget the genius bit—what you want is a human being, a 'mensch,' not a genius." Do you agree?

2. What do you believe are your parents' goals for you? How are they helping you to accomplish them?

3. What are some modern-day obligations that you believe parents should have as duties to their children?

4. What things have your parents taught you that you probably would never have learned in school?

5. Read the lyrics of this famous song by Harry Chapin, "Cat's in the Cradle." How does this song relate to parenting, and are there messages in the song that are directly related to any of the sayings of the rabbis? If so, what are they?

> A child arrived just the other day
> He came to the world in the usual way.
> But there were planes to catch and bills to pay
> He learned to walk while I was away,
> He was talkin' before I knew it,
> And as he grew he was saying:
> "I'm gonna be like you, Dad.
> You know I'm gonna be like you."
>
> Well my son turned ten just the other day.
> He said, "Thanks for the ball, Dad, c'mon let's play.
> Can you teach me to throw?"
> I said, "Not today; I got a lot to do."
> He said, "That's okay" and
> He walked away, but his smile never dimmed.
> I said, "I'm gonna be like him, yeah
> You know, I'm gonna be like him."

Well I've long since retired and my son's moved away
I called him up just the other day.
I said, "I'd like to see you if you don't mind."
He said, "I'd love to Dad if I could find the time."
"You see, my new job's a hassle and the kids have the flu,
But it's sure nice talking to you, Dad,
It's been sure nice talking to you."

And as he hung up the phone it occurred to me
He'd grown up just like me—
My boy was just like me.

7. E. Kent Hayes, in his book *Why Good Parents Have Bad Kids* (Doubleday), defines several characteristics of good parenting. They include:

    1. Providing structure in the home

    2. Becoming actively involved in their child's interests

    3. Working hard to communicate with their children

    4. Recognizing and rewarding their child's positive behavior

    5. Liking themselves and knowing how to laugh

    6. Teaching their children from an early age

    7. Teaching their children the joy in being a part of a larger community

What are your thoughts on these characteristics of good parenting? What are some additional attributes that you believe make for good parenting? List them below:

_____

_____

_____

_____

_____

HEALTH

בְּרִיאוּת

**Exercise removes the harm
caused by most bad habits.**
(Maimonides, *Preservation of Youth*)

What Does Judaism Have to Say?

In Judaism, God is the ultimate owner of
everything, including our bodies. God loans them to
people for the duration of their lives and takes them back
at the time of death. This underlying principle that God
owns people's bodies creates obligations on the part of
people. These obligations include taking care of our
bodies, practicing good and proper hygiene, sleep,
exercise, and diet. Interestingly, according to Jewish law, a
Jew may not live in a city where there is no physician
(*Jerusalem Talmud*, 66d).

God's ownership of our bodies is also behind Jewish
obligation to help other people escape sickness, injury, and
death. Even the duty of a physician to heal the sick is a
function of the divine imperative that God needs help from
humans to preserve and protect what is His.

Quotations on Health

A. The Body

1. Since it is the will of the Almighty that a person's body
be kept healthy and strong, because it is impossible for a

man to have any knowledge of his Creator when ill, it is therefore his duty to shun anything that may waste the body, and to strive to acquire habits that will help him to become healthy. Thus it is written, "Take good heed of your souls" [*Deuteronomy 4:15*].

(Abridged Code of Jewish Law, chap. 32)

2. Our rabbis, of blessed memory, said: "Which is a short verse upon which all the principles of the Torah depend" [*Talmud Berachot 63a*]? It is Proverbs 3:6: "In all ways we must acknowledge God." This means that in all our actions, even those we do in order to sustain life, we must acknowledge God, and do them for the sake of God's name, the Holy Blessed One. For instance, eating, drinking, walking, sitting, lying down, rising, talking—all acts performed to sustain life should be done for the sake of worshipping our Creator or doing something that will be conducive to the service of God.

(Abridged Code of Jewish Law, chap. 31)

Questions on the Body

1. What in your opinion is the basic premise of the above two texts? How does it compare and contrast with the Greco-Roman view of the body?

2. How do the views of the above two texts compare and contrast with the view of today's popular culture? Which view do you most admire, and why?

3. According to Jewish law, God can and does assert the right to restrict the use of our bodies. This means that a woman who is pregnant and decides to have an abortion does not have sole control over the decision. If you were God, what would be your advice to a pregnant woman who was thinking about having an abortion?

4. A major principle in Jewish medical ethics is that the body is a creation of God, and its pleasures are God-given and ought to be used as a source of holiness. What are some ways in which a Jew can use his or her body for attaining holiness?

B. Healthy Daily Regimens

1. The day and night consist of twenty-four hours. Eight hours of sleep, being one-third of the twenty-four-hour day, are sufficient. These hours should be in the latter part of the night, so that the period between retirement and dawn will embrace eight hours, thus one will rise from sleep before sunrise.

(Condensed Code of Jewish Law)

2. One should not sleep downward or on his back, but lying on his side. One should not go to bed immediately after a meal, but wait three or four hours. One should not sleep during the daytime.

(Condensed Code of Jewish Law)

3. Another rule has been laid down concerning the healthy condition of the body: As long as a person takes plenty of exercise, does not overeat, he will contract no illnesses even though he eats inferior food.

(Condensed Code of Jewish Law)

Questions on Healthy Daily Regimens

1. How does the advice related to healthy daily regimens compare with current medical and health practice?

2. What is your reaction to finding these precepts in the Code of Jewish Law?

C. Diet

1. Overeating is like deadly poison to the human body. Most illnesses that befall man arise from either bad food or excessive eating of good food. Solomon in his wisdom said, "He who guards his mouth and tongue keeps himself clear of trouble" (*Proverbs 21:23*). That is to say, "He who guards his mouth from bad food and excessive eating, and keeps his tongue from unnecessary talk."

(Condensed Code of Jewish Law, chap. 31)

2. It is advisable that a person should become accustomed to having breakfast in the morning.

(Condensed Code of Jewish Law, chap. 32)

3. A person should not eat meat unless he has a special appetite for it.

(Talmud Chullin 84a)

4. Adam was not allowed to eat meat, for it is stated, "See, I have given you seed-bearing plants that are upon the earth. And to all the animals on the land, to all the birds in the sky, and to everything that creeps on earth. I give all the green plants for food" (*Genesis 1:29–30*). The implication is that the beasts of the earth shall not be for humans to eat.

(Talmud Sanhedrin 59b)

5. A person who eats food that does not agree with him transgresses three commandments, in that he has despised himself, despised the foods, and recited an improper blessing.

(Talmud Avot de Rabbi Natan 26)

6. In general, a healthy, strong person should eat twice a day, and the feeble and the aged should eat little at a time, several times during the day. The ordinary length of time for the digestion of food for people who eat moderately and have moderate exercise, is six hours. It is best to omit one meal during the week in order that the stomach may have a rest from its work, thus strengthening its digestive power. And it would seem that this omission should take place on Friday [to enjoy the Friday evening meal].

(Condensed Code of Jewish Law, chap. 32)

7. Water is the natural drink for a person, and it is healthful. If the water is clean and pure, it is helpful in that it preserves the moisture of the body and hastens the ejection of waste.

(*Condensed Code of Jewish Law, chap. 32*)

Questions on Diet

1. Why do you think the rabbis were so concerned about the diet of a person? Are you surprised by all of the rabbinic advice related to diet?

2. How do the ancient dietary notions compare with modern dietary ones? Are there contemporary parallels? If you see differences, what are they, and to what do you attribute them?

D. Exercise

1. Anyone who sits around idly and takes no exercise will be subject to physical discomforts and failing strength, even though he eats wholesome food and takes care of himself in accordance with medical advice.

(*Condensed Code of Jewish Law, chap. 31*)

2. Exercise removes the harm caused by most bad habits, which most people have. And no movement is as beneficial, according to the physicians, as body movements and exercise.

(Maimonides, *Preservation of Youth*)

3. It is a known rule in medical science that before eating, a person should have some exercise, by walking or by working until his body becomes warm, and thereafter eat. And concerning this it is written, "With the sweat of your face you shall eat bread (*Genesis 3:19*)." And again, "And the bread of idleness she does not eat (*Proverbs 31:27*)."

(*Condensed Code of Jewish Law, chap. 32*)

4. One should not sit or recline on the left side during a meal. One should not walk, ride, exert himself, shake, or take a walk until the food is digested.

(Mishneh Torah, Fundamentals of the Torah, chap. 4)

Questions on Exercise

1. Why do you think the rabbis cautioned that a person should not recline on the left side during a meal?

2. How do the rabbinic sources on exercise view the importance of exercise?

3. How do these Jewish laws relate to modern notions of exercise and fitness?

ECOLOGY

בַּל תַּשְׁחִית

Your welfare depends on the land
as much as it depends on the welfare of the land.
(Deuteronomy 11:13-17)

What Does Judaism Have to Say?

The ancient rabbis comment in the Midrash that, following the creation of human beings, God took Adam and Eve on a tour of the Garden of Eden to see its beauty and then said to them, "See how beautiful is My handiwork. I have created all of it for you to use. Please take care of it. Do not spoil or destroy my world" (*Ecclesiastes Rabbah 7:13*). This story really reflects the text taken from Deuteronomy: "When you wage war against a city, and you have to besiege it in order to capture it, do not destroy its trees, wielding an ax against them. You may eat from them, but you must not cut them down" (*Deuteronomy 20:19*). The rabbinic principle here is the religious obligation and mitzvah known as *bal tashchit,* "do not destroy." From the verse that forbids the cutting down of fruit-bearing trees, the rabbis of the Talmud extended the principle to prohibiting willful destruction of any object from which someone might benefit.

Perhaps one of the most remarkable things about the relationship between nature and human beings can be found in the midst of Shabbat. We were given six days to manage the earth, to engage in the process of interfering with the natural order of things. But on the holy Sabbath we are instructed neither to create nor to destroy. Instead, on the Sabbath we are required simply to enjoy the beauty of the universe, refrain from "working" the earth, and enjoy the beauty of nature and acknowledge God as its Creator.

Just as the Sabbath provides us with a balance for the work week, Jewish agricultural laws related to what is called the "sabbatical year" provide for the needs of the land. The Bible declares that a Jewish farmer is permitted to sow and reap for six years, but the seventh year is set aside as a sabbath of rest so that the earth may be replenished with nutrients (*Exodus 23:10–11*).

In recent years the growth of industry has given us many new products, but they have come at the cost of cutting down trees, destroying farmland, polluting the air, and dumping toxic waste into our rivers and streams. The message of the rabbinic thinkers is a clear and concise one: the earth belongs to God; as God's people, we are merely caretakers of the earth. The earth is on loan to us, so to speak, and it is our responsibility as Jews to take care of it and preserve it for all the generations yet to come.

Quotations on Ecology

A. Do Not Destroy

1. When you besiege a city for a long time in order to capture it, you must not destroy its trees by wielding an ax against them. You may eat from them, but you must not cut them down. Are trees of the field human to withdraw before you into the besieged city? Only trees that you know do not yield food may be destroyed.

(Deuteronomy 20:19–20)

2. The law of *bal tashchit* forbids you from cutting down your enemies' fruit trees or changing the course of a stream so that trees wither and die. Not only a person who cuts down trees that bear fruit or nuts, but also anyone who smashes household goods, demolishes a building, stops up a spring, or destroys food, transgresses the law of *bal tashchit*.

(Mishneh Torah, Book of Judges,
"Laws of Kings and Wars," 6:8, 10)

3. Whoever destroys anything that could be useful to another person breaks the law of *bal tashchit*.

(Talmud Kodashim 32a)

4. Threshing floors must be kept far enough away from a town to prevent the husks of grain and grasses from polluting the air of the town when the wind blows.

(Mishneh Baba Batra 2:8)

5. A tannery must be built at least 50 cubits (approximately 75 feet) outside a town and must be located only on the east side (downwind) of the town so that foul odors are not carried into the town by the wind.

(Talmud Baba Batra 2:9)

6. Bury your sewage away from the area in which people live, and bury it deep so that it will not cause harm to anyone walking by it.

(Deuteronomy 23:13-15;
Mishneh Torah, "Laws of Kings and Wars," 6:14-15)

7. Rabbinic rulings that helped ensure a safe and healthy environment included bans against polluting drinking water (*Talmud Baba Metzia 11*) and against smoke, dust, bad smells, and noise.

(Mishnah Baba Batra, chap. 2)

8. Do not dump waste in any place from which it could be scattered by the wind or spread by flooding.

(Mishneh Torah, "Tamid and Musaf Offerings" 2:15)

9. Furnaces and other causes of smoke, odor, and air pollution are not permitted inside a city.

(*Talmud Baba Kamma 82b*)

10. While it is the practice to cut one's clothing on hearing of the death of a close relative [this is called "cutting *keriah*"], tearing too much or too many garments violates this principle.

(*Talmud Baba Kamma 91b*)

11. Whoever tears garments in anger, breaks vessels in anger, and scatters money in anger, regard that person as an idolater.

(*Talmud Shabbat 105b*)

12. "Do not destroy anything" is the first call of God, which comes to you, humanity, when you realize yourself as master of the earth. God's call proclaims to you "If you destroy, if you ruin, at that moment you are not human, you are an animal, and you have no right to the things around you. I lent them to you for wise use only. Never forget that I lent them to you."

(Samson Raphael Hirsch,
Horeb: A Philosophy of Jewish Law and Observances)

13. Major General Abraham Yaffee, an Israeli tank commander, once ordered an entire encampment to pull up stakes and move to another location in order to avoid the trampling of a field of rare wild flowers. Another time the Major General halted his tank and ordered a cease-fire to allow a rare bird, a cream colored courser, to cross the path and move out of harm's way.

(Lewis G. Regenstein,
Replenish the Earth)

Questions on Do Not Destroy

1. Deuteronomy 20 asks the question: "Are trees of the field human?" In what ways do you think trees are similar to human beings? How do they differ?

2. From your reading of the quotations, how do the rabbis move from the biblical prohibition against the destruction of trees during war to a general prohibition of wastefulness?

3. In the Talmud Shabbat 105, the tearing of garments and vessels is compared to idolatry. Why do you think such a comparison was made? Do you agree with it?

4. In the above quotations from *Mishneh Torah,* Maimonides enumerated a number of actions that waste our resources and are therefore prohibited. What are some things that you would add to his list? Should driving a car that is not fuel-efficient be a prohibition in Jewish law?

5. The excerpt in the quotation by S. R. Hirsch allows for destruction that occurs as a necessary consequence of what he calls "wise use." How would you go about determining what constitutes "wise use"?

6. What are some ways in which we waste natural resources in our homes, schools, and synagogues?

7. Some environmentalists have said that all of a person's actions have consequences that will affect the environment. Do you agree?

8. The mitzvah of *bal tashchit* teaches us the importance of not being wasteful. In the spaces below jot down some suggestions you might make to others to prevent them from wasting things:

_____

_____

_____

_____

_____

_____

9. What in your estimation is more important: saving a forest of 1,000 acres or cutting the trees for a housing development that would provide many jobs for lumberjacks and builders? List the advantages and disadvantages of such a project.

Advantages	Disadvantages
_____	_____
_____	_____
_____	_____
_____	_____
_____	_____
_____	_____

10. Choose a classmate as your partner and, using the chart below, construct ways you will change your behavior in order to consume fewer resources each day.

Resource	What You Can Do to Preserve
_____	_____
_____	_____
_____	_____
_____	_____
_____	_____

11. In what ways does your room at home (or rooms in school) reflect the principle of *bal tashchit?* What have you done lately to help preserve this principle?

12. Compose a series of contemporary guidelines for Jews concerned with the principle of *bal tashchit.* Divide the guidelines into two sections: acts which an individual should/should not do in his or her personal life, and strategies for dealing with the issues of *bal tashchit* that extend beyond the actions of individuals (e.g., environmental pollution by large companies).

B. Caring for the Earth

To the ancient Israelites, the earth itself was alive. Although there is no ancient word for "environment" or "ecology," there was a Jewish belief that a good life depended on preserving the land. For hundreds of years, rabbis have taught the importance of planting trees to preserve the earth, knowing that trees assist the air, soil, and water and that from trees and plants come many medicines beneficial to humankind.

1. Your welfare depends on the land just as much as does the welfare of the land.

(Deuteronomy 11:13–17)

2. One generation goes and one generation comes, but the earth remains forever.

(Ecclesiastes 1:4)

3. Replenish the earth.

(Genesis 1:28)

4. Land, like humans and animals, must have a time of rest, to renew itself. Six years you shall plant your field but in the seventh you shall neither plant nor reap. It shall be a complete rest for the land.

(Leviticus 25:2–5)

5. Be careful that you do not ruin my world, because if you ruin it, no one will come along to set it right again.

(Ecclesiastes Rabbah, chap. 7)

6. Even if the land is full of good things, you must still plant...even if you are old, you must plant.

(Midrash Tanchuma Kodashim 8)

7. If a person kills a tree before its time, it is as though a soul has been murdered.

(Rabbi Nachman of Bratslav)

8. If not for the trees, human life could not exist.

(Midrash Sifre to Deuteronomy 20:19)

9. Rabbi Yochanan ben Zakkai used to say, "If you have a sapling in your hand and you are told that the Messiah has come, first plant the sapling and then go and welcome the Messiah."

(Avot de Rabbi Natan 31b)

10. It is forbidden to live in a town in which there is no garden or greenery.

(Jerusalem Talmud Kodashim 4:12)

11. One who buys a tree from a friend for felling shall cut it in such a way that the stump remains from which a new tree can grow.

(Talmud Baba Batra 80b)

12. Talmudic Story about a Tree: A rabbi was passing through a field when he noticed an elderly man who was planting an acorn.

"Why are you planting that acorn?" he asked. "You surely do not expect to live long enough to see it grow into an oak tree."

The man replied, "My grandparents planted seeds so that I might enjoy the shade and the fruit trees. Now I do likewise for my grandchildren and all those who come after me."

(Talmud Taanit 23a)

13. The world is a tree and human beings its fruit.

(Solomon ibn Gabirol)

14. It is said that on Tu B'Shevat an angel taps every plant on its head and says, "Grow!"

(*Genesis Rabbah 10:6*)

15. The righteous will flourish like a palm tree and grow mighty like a cedar in Lebanon.

(*Psalm 92:13*)

Questions on Caring for the Earth

1. In your opinion, was the world made for us, or were we made for it? Or were, we, perhaps, made for each other?

What Do You Think?

2. Do human beings bear the sole responsibility for the quality of life on earth?

3. Does the statement in the midrash of Ecclesiastes Rabbah, "Do not ruin my world" mean "Leave it as it is"? In your opinion, is land that is untouched by human activity always better than inhabited land in some way?

4. How can observing Shabbat make any difference in how we treat the environment throughout the rest of the week?

5. What did Rabbi Nachman of Bratslav mean by his statement, "If a person kills a tree before its time, it is as though a soul has been murdered"?

6. Solomon ibn Gabirol wrote, "The world is a tree and human beings its fruit." In what ways is the world like a tree and humans its fruit? Do you agree with his statement?

7. The Torah has been called "a Tree of Life." Why is the Torah in Jewish tradition compared to a tree?

8. What is the connection in Psalm 92 between palm and cedar trees and righteous people?

9. Jewish mystics believed that the outer world of nature is a mirror of people's inner nature. In what way do you think that the more you learn about nature, the more you can know about yourself?

10. In what ways does God show His power in nature and in the environment? Can you think of some prayers that reflect and acknowledge God's power as related to nature?

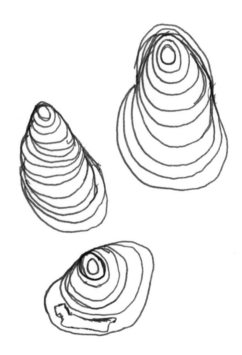

KINDNESS TO ANIMALS

צַעַר בַּעֲלֵי חַיִּים

Do not plow with an ox
and a donkey together in the same yoke.
(*Deuteronomy 22:10*)

What Does Judaism Have to Say?

As far back as bible times, laws were developed to teach
people the need to be compassionate toward animals. In
the Noah story, for example, one of the so-called Noachide
laws (those laws meant to be followed by Jews and non-
Jews alike) prohibits the eating of meat taken from a live
animal, a common practice among pagans. Also, the
religious obligation to observe the Sabbath was extended to
animals as well: oxen, cattle and donkeys.

The rabbis of ancient times, too, spoke at great
length about the responsibility that humans have for
animals. At a time in history when animals undoubtedly
were treated very cruelly by other peoples, the sages
elaborated upon the mitzvah of *tzaar baalei chayim*, literally
"compassion for the pain of living creatures."

One of the most insightful and compelling talmudic
instructions concerning the treatment of animals is found
in the following statement, appearing in Berachot 40a:
"You must not eat your own meal until you have seen to it
that all of your animals are properly fed."

Quotations on Kindness to Animals

1. When an ox, sheep, or goat is born, it should stay with its mother for seven days. From the eighth day on, it is acceptable as an offering by fire to God. However, no animal from the herd or flock can be slaughtered on the same day with its young.

(Leviticus 22:27–28)

2. Do not cook a kid in its mother's milk.

(Exodus 23:19, 34:26; Deuteronomy 14:21)

3. When you see your enemy's donkey lying under its load and would like to leave it alone, you must nevertheless help it to get on its feet.

(Exodus 23:5)

4. If you chance upon a bird's nest in a tree or on the ground, and the nest has young birds or even eggs, and the mother is sitting with her young, do not take the mother together with her children. Let the mother go and take only the young—so that you may fare well and live a long life.

(Deuteronomy 22:6)

5. Do not plow with an ox and a donkey together in the same yoke.

(Deuteronomy 22:10)

6. If an animal falls into a ditch on the Sabbath, place pillows and bedding under it [since it cannot be moved until the end of the Sabbath].

(Talmud Shabbat 128b)

7. *Talmudic Lesson on Compassion*

Rabbi Judah the Prince observed a calf as it was being led to the slaughterhouse. The animal broke away from the herd and hid itself under Rabbi Judah's clothing, crying for mercy. But Judah pushed it away, saying, "Go. This is your destiny." They said in heaven, "Since he showed no compassion, we will bring suffering to him." For many years after this act, Rabbi Judah suffered a series of painful illnesses. One day, Judah's servant was sweeping the house. She was about to sweep away some young weasels which she found on the floor. "Leave them alone," Judah said to his housekeeper. Subsequently they spoke of Judah this way in heaven, "Since he has shown compassion to these rodents, we will be compassionate with him," and he was cured of his illness.

(Talmud Baba Metzia 85a)

8. No person may buy a beast, an animal or a bird until that person has provided food for it.

(Jerusalem Talmud Yevamot 15:3)

9. Jewish people must avoid plucking feathers from live geese, because it is cruel to do so.

(Code of Jewish Law, Even HaEzer, 5:14)

10. When animals lose their young, they suffer great pain. There is no difference between human pain and the pain of other living creatures.

(Maimonides, *Guide for the Perplexed, 3:48*)

11. In the world to come, God will punish riders who wound their horses with spurs.

(Sefer Chassidim, para. 44)

12. Compassion should be extended to all creatures, neither destroying nor despising any of them. For God's wisdom is extended to all created things: minerals, plants, animals and humans. This is the reason the rabbis warned us against despising food. In this way, a person's pity should be extended to all of the works of the Holy Blessed One, just as in God's wisdom, nothing is to be despised. One should not uproot anything that grows unless it is necessary, nor kill any living thing unless it is necessary. Anyone should choose a good death for them with a knife that has been carefully examined, to have pity on them as much as possible.

(Moses Cordovero, The Palm Tree of Deborah)

Questions

1. Why does the Bible teach that animals should stay with their parents for a period of eight days before they can be offered as sacrifices?

2. The Bible commanded animals to "rest" on the Sabbath. Since we do not often use animals today to help us with our work, in what way do you think this commandment is still applicable?

3. Vegetarians believe that eating meat is an act of cruelty toward animals. What is your opinion?

4. What is your opinion regarding the use of animals for medical research?

5. From your reading of the quotations on the treatment of animals, do you think we should continue to keep animals on display in zoos for the entertainment and enjoyment of people?

6. Do you agree with Maimonides that animals are capable of feeling emotional pain and distress? (You may wish to ask a local veterinarian for his or her opinion, and report your findings to the class.)

7. Do you know anyone who is a vegetarian? If so, speak to this person about his or her reasons for abstaining from eating meat. Perhaps you will have an opportunity to report your findings to the class.

8. According to the Torah, God told Adam and Eve that they were required to eat food only from plants and not from animals. Based on your understanding of the Adam and Eve story, and using your imagination regarding the conversation that might have taken place between God and the first human beings as they learned of the prohibition against eating meat, write your own midrash (legend) in the space below. Read it to the class and then have a discussion.

My Midrash

_____

_____

_____

_____

_____

_____

_____

_____

COMMITMENTS

הִתְחַיְבוּת

A person who makes a promise to God or takes
an oath to do something must carry it out.
(Numbers 30:3)

What Does Judaism Have to Say?

Judaism is a religion of concepts and values which are deeply invested in words. The power of words when spoken in the form of an oath or promise is linked to a belief in God, in whose name that vow is made. No doubt you have heard expressions like "in the name of God" and "I swear to God." Jewish tradition takes these statements very seriously. The Book of Proverbs (*18:21*) states, "Death and life are in the power of the tongue."

Whether we call it a vow or a promise or simply one's word, one must keep a commitment. It is tied to one's belief in God and in God's presence in the world and in our lives. The Torah teaches us that a person who makes a vow, a promise to God, or who takes an oath to do something, must carry out that promise (*Numbers 30:3*).

The third of the Ten Commandments states that we should not utter the name of God in vain. In Exodus 20:7 we learn that one should not make a promise casually, without considering the consequences. The rabbis of ancient times were not at all enthusiastic about people taking oaths. They very much understood the power of promises, writing that "it is better to make no promises at all than to make them even if one is certain of fulfilling them" (*Talmud Chullin 2a*).

One of the best-known statements about promises and vows comes to us on the eve of Yom Kippur, the Day of Atonement, in the form of the Kol Nidre prayer. This unusual declaration specifies that all the promises that we have made to God that have gone unfulfilled are null and void. It has been said that Kol Nidre was originally designed to protect Jews who had been forced to convert to Christianity in order to save their lives. It allowed them to make Christian promises without being fearful that they had turned their backs on Jewish tradition.

The most comprehensive of the Jewish law codes, the *Shulchan Aruch,* which was compiled by Rabbi Joseph Karo in the sixteenth century, devotes a great deal of space to the laws of promises and vows. As an example of how seriously the Jewish community has considered vows over the last few centuries, the following warning, borrowed from the Talmud, opens the chapter on vows in the Code of Jewish Law: "Do not be in the habit of making vows. The one who does make a vow is called wicked."

Quotations on Commitments

1. A person who makes a vow, a promise to God or takes an oath to do something must carry it out.

(*Numbers 30:3*)

2. You shall not swear falsely by the name of God.

(*Exodus 20:7*)

3. It is better to make no promises at all than to make them, even if one is certain of fulfilling them.

(*Talmud Chullin 2a*)

4. Vows are a fence for abstinence.

(*Pirke Avot 3:13*)

5. The making of vows is the doorway to folly.

(Talmud Kallah Rabbati 5)

6. A person who utters a vow places a burden on his [or her] neck.

(Jerusalem Talmud Nedarim 9:1)

7. Be careful what you vow, and do not become habituated to making vows, for if you do get into the habit, in the end, sin will break your oath. Any person who breaks his oath denies God without hope of pardon.

(Tanchuma Mattot 79a)

8. That which cannot be destroyed by fire or by water is destroyable by a false oath.

(Talmud Shevuot 39)

9. What is a desirable oath? If the evil impulse is leading you away from the performance of a commandment, take an oath that you will perform it.

(Zohar ii, 91b)

10. Rabbi Eliezer said: "Yes is an oath and no is an oath."

(Talmud Shevuot 36a)

11. If anyone had taken an oath with his lips and heart agreeing, but he immediately retracted after having bound himself, instantly, within the time required for a single utterance, such as "Peace be to you, Rabbi" [a student's greeting], and said, "This is not an oath" or "I regret it" or "I retract," and such like expression signifying that he has set himself free from the binding oath, he is set free and the oath is removed, for he is like one who has been in error.

(Mishneh Torah, Chapter on Oaths)

12. How are oaths absolved? The person who took the oath should present himself to the distinguished scholar, or to three laymen if no expert is available, and say: "I took an oath concerning this and that, and now I am sorry. Had I known that I might be distressed because of it to such a degree, or that such a thing might happen to me, I would not have taken the oath. Had I known at the time of the oath what I know now, I would not have sworn."

Thereupon the scholar, or the eldest of the three laymen, should say to him, "Have you regretted it?" And he should reply, "Yes." Then he should say to him: "You are set free, you are pardoned," or anything similar in meaning in any language. If, however, he said to him, "Your oath is void," or "Your oath is eradicated," or something similar in meaning, what he said is of no avail, because none except a husband or a father can revoke an oath.

(Mishneh Torah, Chapter on Oaths)

13. One should be extremely careful with youngsters in teaching them to speak the truth without oaths, so that they should not become habituated to frequent swearing. This amounts to a duty resting upon their parents and upon the elementary teachers.

(Mishneh Torah, Chapter on Oaths)

14. If a person has made vows in order to adjust his characteristic traits and to improve his behavior, he is indeed alert and deserves praise. Examples: One who was a glutton forbade himself meat for a year or two; or one who was addicted to drinking denied himself wine for a long time, or vowed never to become intoxicated. So too, the one who ran after bribes, hastening to get rich, forbade to himself the gifts or the favors coming from the residents of a particular town.

(Mishneh Torah, Chapter on Vows)

Questions

1. How often do you find yourself vowing a vow or making a promise?

2. Did you ever make a promise that you knew you could not keep? What prompted you to do so? Are there any times that we can make promises about things that we have no intention of keeping?

3. Did you ever make a promise that you wanted to keep but were unable to do so? How did you feel? What did you do to remedy the situation?

4. What do you think should happen to people who do not keep their promises?

5. Why do you believe that Jewish tradition continues to discourage people from making vows and promises?

6. Why are promises so difficult to keep? Think about several promises that God made to the Israelites in the Bible? Did God fulfill these promises?

7. Here are the words of the Kol Nidre prayer. After reading it, see if you can compose your own modern rendition of this ancient prayer.

> All vows, promises, obligations, and oaths to God wherewith we have vowed, sworn, and bound ourselves from this Day of Atonement till the next Day of Atonement, may it come to us for good; lo, of all these, we repent us in them. They shall be absolved, released, annulled, made void, and of none effect. They shall not be binding nor shall they have any power. Our vows to God shall not be vows, and our bonds shall not be bonds, and our oaths shall not be oaths.

My Modern Version

_____

_____

_____

_____

_____

_____

8. Taking an Oath: This story appears in the book *Sefer Chasidim*. After reading the story, discuss the teachings related to taking vows. Do you agree or disagree with them?

It happened that gentiles once falsely accused a Jew of a crime. The Jew was put on trial and was required to take an oath. He swore truthfully, declaring himself innocent of the charges. Afterwards he said to the rabbi, "Although I told the truth, I regret taking the oath and uttering God's Name. You see, my father and mother never took an oath—even a true oath—as long as they lived. I was compelled to swear, and I did it against my will, since otherwise I would have been condemned to death."

The rabbi answered, "If you want to atone for this, you should resolve never again to utter God's Name, either to affirm a true statement or in vain, either in German or in any other language, as people are in the habit of saying, 'May God help us.' Don't use such expressions. Enunciate God's Name only when you are reading biblical verses. Do not do business with a person unless you can trust him without having to resort to taking an oath, so that you will not be drawn into a situation where you will have to swear."

REMEMBRANCE

**We Jews are a community
by virtue of historic memory.**
(Martin Buber)

What Does Judaism Have to Say?

The gift of memory allows the Jewish people to fulfill many obligations related to memory and remembrance. Each and every day in the Jewish liturgy, Jewish worshippers are asked to remember the verse that first appears in the Ten Commandments: "I am the Lord your God Who brought you out of the land of Egypt and out of slavery." Of course, this theme of "from slavery to freedom" is the major component of the Passover Haggadah.

The Jewish New Year, Rosh Hashanah, is also called "Yom Hazikaron"—the Day of Remembrance. On this day Jews gather to remember God as Creator of the world. And on this day God is said to remember the deeds of His people.

One very special Sabbath, the one immediately preceding the festival of Purim, is called the Sabbath of Remembrance, or *Shabbat Zachor.* On this Sabbath the Torah reading concludes with a special portion whose opening words are, "Remember what Amalek did to you by the way as you came forth out of Egypt." In effect, this phrase has served as a battle cry for the Jewish people to recognize the anti-Semite and to prevent that person from performing evil.

The memorial service, known as *Yizkor* (may God remember), which is the first word of the prayer traditionally said, was originally held only on Yom Kippur, the Day of Atonement, in order to stir the people to repentance. Since the eighteenth century, however, Yizkor memorial services have been conducted also on the last day of Passover, the second day of Shavuot, and the eighth day of Sukkot, which is Shemini Atzeret. The Yizkor prayer, like the anniversary of a death (*yahrzeit*), presents a stirring emotional appeal to modern Jews to remember all of their loved ones and to pledge deeds of kindness in their memory.

Quotations on Remembrance

1. Remember the Sabbath day to keep it holy.

(*Exodus 20:8*)

2. We Jews are a community by virtue of historic memory. We have been held together and upheld by common remembering.

(Martin Buber)

3. The essence of Jewish religious thinking does not lie in entertaining a concept of God, but in the ability to articulate a memory of memories, of illumination by God's Presence.

(Abraham Joshua Heschel)

4. There is a difference between learning one's lesson one hundred times and learning it one hundred and one times.

(*Talmud Chagigah 9b*)

5. Remember us unto life, O King Who delights in life.

(High Holy Day Liturgy)

6. God remembered Noah and every living creature, and all the cattle that were with him in the ark. God made a wind to blow over the earth, and the waters abated.

(Genesis 8:1)

7. God has made a memorial for His wondrous works.

(Psalm 91:5)

8. There is a time for everything under the sun a time to forget, and a time to remember.

(Sim Shalom Prayerbook, Yizkor Memorial Service)

9. "That you may look upon it and remember" (*Numbers 15:39*). Looking leads to remembering, and remembering leads to doing.

(Tanchuma Shelach)

10. One who listens to the rabbis and remembers their words is like a rabbi himself.

(Talmud Berachot 47)

11. Remembrance brings action in its train.

(Talmud Menachot 13)

12. In remembering is the secret of redemption.

(Nachman of Bratslav, written on entrance to Yad Va-Shem Holocaust Memorial, Jerusalem)

Questions

1. What are some of your earliest recollections of events in your life? What is there about these events that you continue to remember them?

2. What did Nachman of Bratslav mean when he said, "In remembering is the secret of redemption"? Do you agree with this statement?

3. What are the ways in which one can remember the Sabbath day, in order to keep it holy?

4. What is meant by the talmudic verse from tractate Chagigah, "There is a difference between learning one's lesson one hundred times and learning it one hundred and one times"?

5. Why do you believe that in the prayerbook we are repeatedly enjoined to remember that God took us out of the land of Egypt to be our God?

6. What are the things in life that you believe you are most likely to remember? What are some ways of keeping these memories alive for others as well?

7. The Yiddish writer Jacob Abramowitz once said, "Among Jews, a birthday is no holiday, but the anniversary of a death, *that* a Jew remembers." What do you suppose Abramowitz meant by his statement, and do you agree with it?

8. Memorial Day in the United States has become extremely commercialized, with innumerable advertisements for sales of clothing and other merchandise. What are your suggestions for making Memorial Day a truer day of remembrance?

9. The Torah attaches great important to the wearing of *tzitzit* (fringes) as a visible reminder of the obligation to keep the divine commandments: "When you look upon the fringe, you will remember to do all the commands of God." Do you think that the *tallit* (prayershawl) succeeds in reminding the person who wears it of his or her obligations to keep divine commandments? If you were to create a ritual or a ritual item that would help a Jew always to remember his or her responsibility, what would your creation be? Describe it.

REPENTANCE

תְּשׁוּבָה

Great is repentance, because for the sake
of the one who truly repents,
the whole world is pardoned.
(Talmud Yoma 86b)

What Does Judaism Have to Say?

The Hebrew term for repentance is *teshuvah,* meaning
"return." In Judaism, a person can get back on the right
track, if he or she chooses to return to God, by restoring
the proper relationship of respect for God. This theme of
returning was a favorite one of the Israelite prophets. For
example, the prophet Hosea speaks to the Israelites and
says, "Return, O Israel, to your God." The prophet
Jeremiah warns, "Return, you backsliding Israel."
Repentance requires a concerted effort on the part of the
sinner to break with the past and return to better ways.

The great medieval philosopher Maimonides
devotes ten chapters to repentance in his work the *Mishneh
Torah.* Defining different grades of repentance, he offers
this illustration: "An opportunity presents itself for
repeating an offense, and the offender, while *able* to
commit the offense, nevertheless refrains from doing so
because he is penitent, and not out of fear or failure of
vigor. If however, a person only repents in old age, at a
time when he is no longer capable of doing what he used
to do, this is not an excellent mode of repentance
[nevertheless] he is accepted as a penitent." Even if one
transgressed all his life and only repented on the day of his

death, according to Maimonides that person's transgressions are pardoned.

Quotations on Repentance

1. A twinge of conscience in a person's heart is better than all the flogging that such a person may receive.

(Talmud Berachot 7)

2. Rabbi Eliezer ben Hyrcanus said, "Repent one day before your death." His students asked him, "How is it possible for a person to repent one day before his death, since a person does not know when he shall die?" He replied, "All the more reason is there that a person should repent every day, lest he die the next day. Thus, all his days will be days of repentance."

(Talmud Avot de Rabbi Natan 15)

3. Rabbi Simeon ben Lakish said, "Repentance induced by fear of consequences causes willful sins to be treated as unwitting. Repentance that springs from a nobler motive— love of God—causes willful sins to be treated as righteous deeds."

(Talmud Yoma 86b)

4. If a person repents and returns to sinning, that is no repentance.

(Pesikta Rabbati 44)

5. Rabbi Meir said, "Great is repentance, because for the sake of one who truly repents, the whole world is pardoned."

(Talmud Yoma 86b)

6. In the place where penitents stand, even the wholly righteous cannot stand.

(Talmud Berachot 34b)

7. One must not say to a person who has repented [and changed his way of life], "Remember your former transgressions."

(Talmud Baba Metzia 58b)

8. Consider every day your last, and you will always be ready with good deeds and repentance.

(Talmud Shabbat 153a)

9. The gates of prayer are sometimes open, sometimes closed, but the gates of repentance are open forever.

(Deuteronomy Rabbah 2:7)

10. Woe to a person who is not aware of his/her faults, for such a person does not know what he/she needs to correct. Double woe to a person who is not aware of his or her virtues, for such a person lacks the tools to correct himself or herself.

(Rabbi Yerucham Liebovitz)

11. As long as the candle is still burning, it is still possible to make repairs.

(Israel Salanter)

12. There are three requisites for repentance: seeing eyes, hearing ears, and an understanding heart, ready to return and be healed. Let your eyes see your conduct; let your ears hear words of admonition by our holy rabbis; and let your heart understand its eternal purpose. Then you will attain perfect repentance.

(Rabbi Nachman of Bratslav)

13. All sins are atoned for by repentance, except such as entail irretrievable harm—such as corrupting, misleading and misinforming a multitude, ruining the reputation of an innocent person, and keeping misappropriated articles.

(Saadia Gaon)

14. Because piety is a difficult way of life to adopt, it is good to start when you are young. The repentance of an old man whose desire is gone is like a man who wants to indulge in slander but his speech is impaired and he is unable to communicate. The most admirable kind of repentance is when a person still possesses his strength and vigor, and his passion threatens to overwhelm him, but he subdues it. By controlling his intensely strong desire, he really is performing a powerful feat. If you are faced with a difficult task and you carry it out in spite of all obstacles, your reward is very great.

(Sefer Chasidim, para. 7)

15. The repentant sinner should strive to do good with the same faculties with which he sinned. With whatever part of the body he sinned, he should now engage in good deeds. If his feet had run to sin, let them now run to the performance of the good. If his mouth had spoken falsehood, let it now be opened in wisdom. Violent hands should now open in charity. The troublemaker should now become a peacemaker.

(Jonah Gerondi, *Gates of Repentance*)

16. Rabbi Simcha Bunam once asked his students, "How can we tell when a sin we have committed has been pardoned?"

His students gave various answers but none of them pleased the rabbi.

"We can tell," he said, "by the fact that we no longer commit that sin."

(Martin Buber)

Questions

1. *Pirke Avot (2:1)* states that when a person thinks about three things, he or she will not be overcome with the desire to sin: Know what is above: a seeing eye, an ear that hears, and a book in which all your actions are recorded. In the space provided, write your own modern version of things that will help overcome one's desire to sin.

Modern Version: A person will not be overcome with the desire to sin when

_____

_____

_____

_____

2. What in your opinion is the most difficult part of repenting when you realize that you have wronged another person? How successful have you been in repentance in such a case? Were you forgiven by the one that you wronged?

3. What in your opinion is the best proof that one is truly penitent?

4. Perfect repentance has been described by a variety of rabbinic thinkers in different ways. What is your description of perfect repentance?

5. The ten days between Rosh Hashanah and Yom Kippur are known as the *Aseret Y'may Teshuvah*, the Ten Days of Repentance. These are solemn days, generally to be marked by contrition and prayers for divine forgiveness. Have you ever used these special days to repent for your mistakes? If so, describe your experience.

6. How to Repent

Read the following story by Rabbi Judah ben Asher. What does this story have to teach regarding repentance? What is the moral of the story?

It is told that once there was a wicked man who committed all kinds of sins. One day he asked a wise man to teach him an easy way to repent, and the latter said to him, "Refrain from telling lies." He went forth happily, thinking that he could follow the wise man's advice and still go on as before. When he decided to steal, as had been his custom, he reflected, "What will I do in case someone asks me, 'Where are you going?' If I tell the truth, 'To steal,' I shall be arrested. If it tell a lie, I shall be violating the command of this wise man." In the same manner he reflected on all other sins, until he repented with a perfect repentance.

7. Rabbi Eliezer ben Hyrcanus advised people to be in the habit of repenting each day. Do you feel it is possible to repent daily? If so, how?

8. Rabbi Meir said that when one truly repents, the entire world is pardoned. What do you believe he meant by this statement?

9. What are some ways that you have made amends between yourself and God?

10. The Baal Shem Tov once wrote, "If a man has beheld evil, he may know that it was shown for him in order that he learn his own guilt and repent; for what is shown to him is also within him." What do you think the Baal Shem Tov meant by this statement? Do you agree with it?

RESPECT FOR THE ELDERLY

הֲדוּר פְּנֵי זָקֵן

**Even in old age they shall bear fruit,
they shall be full of vigor and strength.
(Psalm 92:15)**

What Does Judaism Have to Say?

Consider the words of Leviticus 19:32: "Rise before the aged and show respect to the elderly." This biblical passage instructs us to treat older adults with respect. It is often posted in Israeli buses to encourage people to offer their seats to the elderly. Throughout Jewish history, the elders were sought for advice because they had participated in so many of life's experiences. Indeed, the whole philosophy of care for the aged is expressed in the poignant cry of Psalm 71:9: "Cast me not off in the time of old age. When my own strength fails, do not forsake me."

When the aged needed support to live independently and the family lacked the necessary resources, the Jewish community always came to the rescue and provided assistance. Yet it was not until modern times that these elderly capable of independence were treated as a group separate from the sick and the poor in the community. Thus, societies for the aged and homes for the elderly developed in North America in the nineteenth century. The first Jewish home for the aged in the United States was established in St. Louis in 1855. Today most cities that boast of substantial Jewish communities have care facilities for the elderly. Many synagogues and Jewish community centers today have special programs for older adults, providing them with continued opportunities for study, socializing, and continued growth as human beings and as contributing members of the Jewish community.

Quotations on Respect for the Elderly

1. How welcome is old age. The aged are beloved by God.

(Exodus Rabbah 5:12)

2. Even the chirping of a bird awakens the aged.

(Talmud Shabbat 152)

3. Rabbi Joshua ben Levi said: "Honor and respect the elderly and saintly scholar, whose physical powers are broken, equally with the young and vigorous one. For the stone tablets that were broken, no less than the whole ones, had a place in the Ark of the Covenant."

(Talmud Berachot 8b)

4. Rabbi Jose the Galilean said, "'To honor the aged' means that one should not sit in the seat of an elderly person, nor speak before he has spoken, nor contradict him."

(Talmud Kiddushin 32b)

5. Even in old age they shall bear fruit, they shall be full of vigor and strength.

(Psalm 92:15)

6. The prosperity of a country is in accordance with its treatment of the aged.

(Nachman of Bratslav)

Questions

1. The Bible teaches us that the commandment to "love your neighbor as yourself" is one of the most important mitzvot in the Torah. How do you go about fulfilling it when "your neighbor" is elderly?

2. In the Passover Haggadah we are told that when Rabbi Elazar ben Azariah was seventeen years old he said , "I appear like a person who is seventy years old." What do you think motivated him to say this? What do you think he had in mind? Do his words reflect a positive or a negative attitude toward growing older?

3. How do you feel about the way in which the elderly today are portrayed in movies and on television? Is there, in your opinion, stereotyping of the elderly?

4. Job 12:12 states that, "With the aged comes wisdom, and length of days brings understanding." Do you agree with this statement? What experiences have you had to support or undermine Job's claim.

5. Reb Nachman of Bratslav taught that "the prosperity of a country is in accordance with its treatment of the aged." Do you agree? Do you feel that the elderly are treated properly in the United States and Canada? What about Israel?

6. Aside from perhaps your relatives, do you have any older adults that you consider your friends? Is it possible for younger adults and older adults to be involved in projects with each other?

7. How do you feel about the so-called retirement communities that do not allow families with children to live there?

8. What is your reaction to this statement appearing in *Pirke Avot 4:25*:

Elisha ben Abuya said, "When a person learns something while still young, it is similar to ink written on new paper. However, when a person learns something as an older person, it is like writing with ink on paper that has already been erased."

9. What kinds of things do a synagogue or Jewish Community Center need to do in order to provide a more supportive environment for older adult members?

10. Rabbi Yossi ben Kisma expressed the hardship of old age through this riddle: "Two are better than three, and woe for the one thing that goes and does not return." Can you solve this riddle? To what do you think Rabbi Yossi ben Kisma was referring? What is "the one thing that goes in old age, never to return"?

LOVING ONE'S NEIGHBOR

וְאָהַבְתָּ לְרֵעֲךָ

Love your neighbor as yourself, I am God.
(Leviticus 19:18)

What Does Judaism Have To Say?

According to Rabbi Akiva, "Loving your neighbor as yourself" *(Leviticus 19:18)* is the most important mitzvah in the entire Torah. Two thousand years ago, when a non-Jew challenged Rabbi Hillel to teach him the whole Torah while he stood on one foot, Hillel answered: "What is hateful to you, do not do to your neighbor. That is the entire Torah—all the rest is commentary. Go and learn it" *(Talmud Shabbat 31a)*.

The verse "love your neighbor as yourself" asks us to learn to behave toward others (whether we like them or not) as we would want them to behave toward us. This verse asks us to act properly.

This mitzvah of loving one's neighbor as oneself has been expanded in the codes of Jewish law to include the importance of visiting the sick, comforting the mourner, and even making a bride and groom happy. Concern for one's neighbor includes a concern for his moral and spiritual growth. The Torah *(Leviticus 19:17)* therefore asks us not to simply rebuke a neighbor who is doing wrong but to keep rebuking until the neighbor mends his ways.

If we do want to warn anyone, we must do so in a kind and gentle manner, always pointing out that we have only one goal in mind: to reach out and extend a helping hand to a friend.

Perhaps it has been our ability to reach out to fellow Jews in need that has helped our people to survive. All Israelites—all Jews—are linked together as brothers and sisters, say the sages.

In modern times, the philosopher Martin Buber built his philosophy called "I–Thou" around the mitzvah of loving one's neighbor, teaching that one should never treat another as a thing or an object, but as a human being like ourselves.

Quotations on Loving Your Neighbor

1. When love is strong, we can lie on the edge of a sword.

(Mishneh Sanhedrin 72)

2. Whoever destroys a single life, it is as if that person had destroyed an entire world.

(Mishneh Sanhedrin 37)

3. What is hateful to you, do not do to your neighbor. This is the whole of Torah. All the rest is commentary.

(Talmud Shabbat 31a)

4. The person who truly loves another can read the other's thoughts.

(The Koretzer Rebbe)

5. Hatred stirs up strife, but love draws a veil over all transgressions.

(Proverbs 10:12)

6. Just as we love ourselves despite the faults we know we have, so should we love our neighbors despite the faults that we see in them.

(Baal Shem Tov)

7. A person should not donate things that are dangerous to the poor. It happened that a person received a pair of shoes that belonged to a poor man who had died. He wanted to donate them to a poor man, but people told him: "Don't do it. Love your neighbor as yourself [because the shoes of a dead person are a bad sign]. You shall rather sell the shoes to avoid endangering the life of a Jew, and give the money to the poor."

(*Sefer Chasidim*)

8. A person should train himself to do two things: first to honor all creatures, in whom he recognizes the exalted nature of the Creator, Who in wisdom created man. And so it is with regard to all creatures. In them is the wisdom of the Creator. He should see for himself that they are therefore exceedingly to be honored, for the Creator of all, the most exalted Wise One, has busied Himself with them and if, God forbid, man despises them, he touches upon the honor of their Creator.

The second is to bring the love of his fellowmen into his heart, even loving the wicked as if they were his brothers and more so until the love of his fellowmen becomes firmly fixed in his heart.

(Moses Cordovero, *The Palm Tree of Deborah*)

9. We must love our neighbor because he is *kamocha,* like us. We must first respect ourselves as unique human beings. Then we can come to have the same regard for our fellow human beings.

(Erich Fromm)

10. To love your fellow human being means putting yourself in his or her position. For instance, in thinking of a friend who is ill one must say, "If I were ill myself, what would be the choicest blessing I could seek from God?" and then pray that the other should receive that blessing.

(Sforno)

Questions

1. In the commandment "Love your neighbor as yourself," God has commanded us to do an action mitzvah that involves a feeling. Do you think love is something that can be willed? Can anyone be instructed or commanded to love?

2. How can we love neighbors, many of whom we may not even know?

3. Think about your neighbors, those who live next door or in the neighborhood. Do you feel that you have fulfilled the mitzvah of loving them as much as you love yourself? Can you do more?

4. In your opinion, does the mitzvah of loving your neighbor as yourself truly mean that you must like everyone?

5. If you have two neighbors and they both need your help, how do you decide which neighbor to help first?

6. What are the various ways in which people show that they care about their neighbors?

7. Which organizations in your community are based on the fundamental principle of loving your neighbor? In what ways do they serve your community?

8. What is your own personal understanding of "Love your neighbor as yourself"?

RIGHTEOUSNESS

צֶדֶק

Tzedakah delivers a person from death.
(Proverbs 10:2)

What Does Judaism Have to Say?

The Hebrew word *tzedakah* is often translated as "charity," but that is really an imprecise definition. The word "charity" is derived from the Latin word *caritas*, referring to the love of one person for another. The word *tzedakah* derives from the Hebrew word *tzedek*, which means "righteousness" or "justice." Thus, Jews are obligated to give not because helping others is a kind thing to do, but because righteous giving helps to eliminate injustice in the world.

Interestingly, giving *tzedakah* is required of all people—rich and poor. No matter where we are in life, there are always people less fortunate than we are. All people should know the joy of giving, of fulfilling this important mitzvah. In rabbinic literature, the act of righteous giving was considered so important that it was equal to the sum of all the other religious obligations.

Charity also was known to have a redemptive aspect to it. The following talmudic story illustrates *tzedakah*'s redemptive value:

Astrologers told Rabbi Akiva that, on the day his daughter is to enter the bridal chamber, a snake would bite her and she would die. As the wedding day approached, Rabbi Akiva became more and more worried. On the day of her marriage, the bride took out a brooch and stuck it into the wall. By chance, the pin penetrated the eye of a poisonous snake. The next morning, when she pulled the brooch from the wall, the dead snake dropped to the ground. Overjoyed that she had survived the fateful night, Rabbi Akiva asked her, "What did you do to be thus saved?" She replied, "A poor man came to our door in the evening while everybody was busy at the banquet. Since there was none to attend to him, I took the portion that was given to me and gave it to him."

"You have done a good deed," he said to her. Thereupon Rabbi Akiva went out and taught: "Charity delivers from death itself." (*Talmud Shabbat 156b*)

One should never expect praise or thanks when giving *tzedakah*. After all, one is only doing what one is supposed to do and nothing more. Centuries ago the prophet Micah told how a person should live righteously: "You have been told, O man, what is good and what God requires of you; only to do justly, love mercy and walk humbly with God" (*Micah 6:8*).

Quotations on Righteousness

1. When you reap the harvest of your land, do not reap the edges of your field. Also, do not gather the gleanings of your harvest. Do not pick your vineyard bare or gather its fallen fruit. Leave them for the poor and the stranger. I am the Lord your God.

(*Leviticus 19:9–10*)

2. Even a poor person who lives on *tzedakah* should practice *tzedakah*.

(*Talmud Gittin 7a*)

3. The blessing of *tzedakah* is greater for the person who gives than for the person who receives.

(Leviticus Rabbah 34:10)

4. The person who gives only a little honestly earned money to *tzedakah* is better than the person who gives lots of money that has been gained through fraud.

(Ecclesiastes Rabbah 4)

5. (There are some people who fall on hard times but are too proud to take charity, even though they need it. In such cases, the mitzvah of giving charity requires one to get money to them some other way, such as lending it to them.)

Our rabbis taught: If a poor man has no money but does not want to let other people support him, one is required to lend him money and then let him have it as a gift. So asserts Rabbi Meir.

The sages say: "At first one is required to give him money as a gift and then to give it to him as a loan.

"How can one be given the money as a gift first if one refuses to accept other people's money?

"Rava explained: At first, the money should be offered to him as a gift. If he doesn't accept it, it should then be offered to him as a loan."

6. The ultimate purpose of the laws of *tzedakah* is to nurture in people the quality of mercy and kindness and not just eliminate poverty. God could have accomplished that by providing for the needs of the poor without human intervention.

(Sefer HaChinnuch 66, Mishpatim)

7. *Tzedakah* delivers a person from death.

(Proverbs 10:2)

8. Hillel used to say, The more *tzedakah,* the more *shalom.*

(Pirke Avot 2:8)

9. Rabbi Yannai once saw someone giving a *zuz* [coin] to a poor man in public. Rabbi Yannai told the giver, "Better not to have given it to him at all than to have given it in a way that embarrassed him."

In the school of Rabbi Shaila it was said: This refers to someone who gives charity to a poor woman in secret, for anyone that notices it might put the wrong interpretation on it.

(Talmud Chagiga 5a)

10. Rabbi Yitzchak said, "Whoever gives even a small coin to a poor man receives six blessings, but whoever speaks reassuringly to him receives eleven blessings."

(Talmud Baba Batra 9b)

11. Rabbi Yochanan said, "The rains are held back only because of those people that pledge money to charity in public but do not actually give it, as it is written, 'As clouds and wind but no rain, so is the man that takes praise in a false gift' [*Proverbs 25:14*]."

(Talmud Taanit 8b)

12. There was a secret chamber in the Temple where pious people would leave money in secret, and those who had been well-to-do would come and take in secret.

(Mishneh Shekalim 5:6)

13. One who lends money is greater than one who performs charity, and one who forms a partnership is greater than all.

(Talmud Shabbat 63a)

14. To give up to a fifth of one's wealth is the most preferable way to perform the mitzvah of *tzedakah*; to give one tenth of one's wealth is a middling way to perform it; to give less than one tenth is looked upon poorly.

(Mishneh Torah, Laws of Gifts for the Poor 7:5)

15. If a person has food in his home and wishes to perform an act of *tzedakah* with it, first he must sustain his father and mother; if there is food remaining, he should sustain his brothers and sisters; after that, the other members of his household; after that, other members of his family; after that, those who dwell in his immediate area; after that, those who dwell in his neighborhood; from then on, he may increase his benevolence among the Jewish people.

(Seder Eliyahu Rabbah)

Questions

1. If you were given $10,000 and told to use it for *tzedakah*, how would you determine what to do with the money?

2. What words describe the way you feel when you give *tzedakah*? To which organizations do you most enjoy giving?

3. The rabbis once said that a person who gives *tzedakah* without anyone knowing about it is greater than Moses. Do you think that someone who gives *tzedakah* anonymously is more commendable than one who wants everyone to know about his or her *tzedakah* gift?

4. *Pirke Avot 5:16* describes four different kinds of people who give *tzedakah*: "The person who wants to give but believes that others should not give. The person who wants others to give but will not give himself. The person who gives and wants others to give. And finally the person who will not give and does not want others to give." What do you think motivates these kinds of attitudes? Do you know people who fit into these categories? What can you do to change their attitude toward giving?

5. The Jewish ideals of *tzedakah* were taught by Moses Maimonides centuries ago. He believed that *tzedakah* is like a ladder. It has eight rungs, from bottom to top. Each step you climb brings you closer to Heaven.

1. The person who gives reluctantly and with regret.

2. The person who gives graciously, but less than one should.

3. The person who gives what one should, but only after being asked.

4. The person who gives before being asked.

5. The person who gives without knowing to whom he or she gives, although the recipient knows the identity of the donor.

6. The person who gives without making his or her identity known.

7. The person who gives without knowing to whom he gives, and with the recipient not knowing from whom he receives.

8. The person who helps another to become self-supporting by a gift or a loan or by finding employment for the recipient.

In the space below try to identify a situation that would demonstrate each of the eight steps of Maimonides:

1._____

2._____

3._____

4._____

5._____

6._____

7._____

8._____

Do you believe that it is really more ethical to give *tzedakah* anonymously than with public fanfare? Do you think that a selfish motivation can negate the merit a person should receive for his or her charitable giving?

> # HONOR
>
> כָּבוֹד
>
> The place does not honor the person;
> The person honors the place.
> (*Talmud Taanit 19b*)

What Does Judaism Have to Say?

Marks of distinction (in Hebrew, *kavod*) accorded to individuals are represented in talmudic literature as tokens of self-respect or honor of self. The word *kavod* has been used to refer to the splendor of God, Who is sometimes referred to in rabbinic literature as *Hakavod*, The Glorious One. God imparts His glory and splendor to those who revere God, especially the prophets and the righteous. Just as God bestows His *kavod,* so too are Jews bidden to show honor to worthy people.

It is natural for people to seek honor from their fellow human beings. However, the rabbis consistently warn that honor cannot be acquired by the one who pursues it. In fact, the more one chases after an honor, the more elusive that honor becomes. Only if one seeks to avoid honor will it pursue him.

One of the most popular pieces of rabbinic advice related to the question of who is honored is that given in *Pirke Avot 4:1*: "Who is honored? One who honors his fellow human beings."

Quotations on Honor

1. Be solicitous for the honor of your colleagues.

(Talmud Berachot 28b)

2. The person who endeavors to gain honor at the price of his fellow human being's degradation has no portion in the World to Come.

(Jerusalem Talmud Chagigah 2:1)

3. Honor departs when it is sought by the undeserving.

(Midrash Psalms 16)

4. The place does not honor the person. The person honors the place.

(Talmud Taanit 19b)

5. There is an obligation to honor any king. This is derived from the biblical verse, "God spoke to Moses and to Aaron, and commanded them concerning the Children of Israel and Pharaoh, to bring the Children of Israel out of Egypt" *(Exodus 6:13)*. Rashi, the medieval commentator, commenting on this verse, explains that God commanded Moses and Aaron to honor Pharaoh.

6. It is a religious duty to honor a person who performs good deeds, even if that person is not wealthy.

(Talmud Kiddushin 33b)

7. Teachers are always honored by having students rise in their presence.

(Code of Jewish Law, Yoreh Deah 244:15)

8. Who is honored? One who honors humankind, for it is written *(Samuel I 2:30)*: "For them that honor Me will I honor, and they that despise Me shall be lightly esteemed."

(Pirke Avot 4:1)

9. Seek not greatness for yourself and do not covet honor.

(Pirke Avot 6:5)

10. Rabbi Jose the Galilean asked, "What is honoring? It means that one should not sit in the seat of an old man, or speak before he has spoken, or contradict him."

(*Talmud Kiddushin 32b*)

11. When Rabbi Nehuniah ben HaKanah was asked by his students, "By what merit have you lived such a long life?" he replied, "I never sought to gain honor at the cost of my fellow man's being degraded, the curse of my fellow man never came with me to my couch, and I have always been liberal with my money."

(*Talmud Megillah 28a*)

Questions

1. Do you know any persons who continually seek honors? Why do you think they do this?

2. What are some ways in which some people gain honor at the expense of their fellow human beings?

3. What kind of person would you most like to see honored? Why?

4. Teachers in ancient times were honored by students' rising in their presence. How do you feel about this kind of an honor for a teacher? Can you think of a situation today involving a teacher or scholar that would merit rising in that person's presence?

5. Proverbs 3:9 says, "Honor God with your wealth." What are some of the ways in which a person can honor God with his or her wealth?

6. Shimon bar Yochai said, "To honor one's parents is even more important than honoring God." What are some ways in which you honor your parents? If you choose to become a parent and are blessed with children, how would you want them to show honor to you?

7. Proverbs 3:9 states: "Honor God with substance. Just as you must honor God even if there is financial loss, you must honor your parents even if you lose money as a result of it." What could you do for God, or your parents, as part of your desire to honor them that might cause you to lose money?

8. How would you define the word "honor"?

9. *Talmud Nedarim 49b* states: "No labor, however humble, dishonors a person." What do you think the Talmud means by this statement?

10. *Talmud Chullin 84b* states that a person should honor his wife and children above his means. What does this statement mean to you? In what way can a person honor his family above his means?

SAVING A LIFE

פִּקּוּחַ נֶפֶשׁ

You shall not stand by the
blood of your neighbor.
(*Leviticus 19:16*)

What Does Judaism Have to Say?

The preservation of human life takes priority over all the other religious obligations in Judaism. When a life is involved, all Sabbath and holy day laws may be suspended to safeguard the individual. Rabbinic thinkers emphasize this principle by citing the following verse from Leviticus 18:5: "You shall keep My laws and ordinances, which if a person does, he shall live by them." The rabbis comment that this means that a person shall live by the laws and not die by them.

There are three instances in which the law takes precedence over life. If the only way one can stay alive is by committing murder, worshipping idols, or committing adultery or incest, one should be prepared to die.

In cases of idolatry and unchastity, the specific application of the talmudic ruling is not always clear. For example, a married woman, who in the normal course of events, is forbidden to have sexual relations with anyone other than her husband, is not expected to resist a rapist if doing so will endanger her life.

When it comes to murder, the law allows no exceptions. A person cannot save his own life, or the life of anyone else, if it means killing an innocent person.

Regarding the keeping of the Sabbath versus saving a human life, all Jewish legal sources have ruled that saving a human life takes precedence over observing the Sabbath. Maimonides, the great medieval philosopher, goes so far as to rule that in those instances when the Sabbath must be violated, it is preferable to have an adult and scholarly Jew, not a minor or non-Jew, do so, "to teach that the purpose of the laws of the Torah is to bring mercy and lovingkindness to the world" (*Mishneh Torah, Laws of the Sabbath*).

In accordance with Maimonides' ruling, an organization consisting mostly of Orthodox Jews called *Hatzalah* (Rescue) has been established in New York City to provide emergency first aid treatment. This rescue squad operates seven days a week, including Shabbat and Jewish festivals.

Jewish law even goes further, allowing its most sacred rituals to be violated where there is only a potential endangerment of life. In 1848 in Vilna, a cholera epidemic broke out, and doctors advised Rabbi Israel Salanter, the leading rabbinic authority, that not only those who were sick but all should eat on the holy day of Yom Kippur, since the fast would lower the people's resistance and increase their risk of contracting the disease. Rabbi Salanter proclaimed that all the Jews should eat on Yom Kippur. He himself also joined in the eating, thus setting the example for all of his followers.

Indeed one might summarize the importance of protecting oneself and one's fellow human beings with the biblical phrase "Choose life!"

Quotations on Saving a Life

1. You shall not stand by the blood of your neighbor.
(*Leviticus 19:16*)

2. The reason that Adam was created alone in the world is to teach that whoever destroys a single soul, the Bible imputes it to him as though such a person had destroyed the entire world.

(Talmud Sanhedrin 37a)

3. Water may be heated on the Sabbath for a sick person.

(Talmud Yoma 84b)

4. The saving of life supersedes the Sabbath.

(Talmud Shabbat 132a)

5. Whoever saves one life, it is as if he saved the entire world.

(Mishnah Sanhedrin 4:5)

6. All Jews are responsible one for another.

(Talmud Shevuot 39a)

7. If a woman is in hard labor, the child in her womb may be cut up and brought out piece by piece, because the mother's survival has priority over that of the child. But if the greater part of the child has already emerged, it may not be touched, since one life may not be sacrificed to preserve another.

(Talmud Ohalot 7:6)

Questions on Saving a Life

1. A Talmudic Dilemma

What is the moral of the following talmudic story:

A man came to Rava and said to him: "The governor of my town has ordered me to kill someone and, if I refuse, he will have me killed. What shall I do?"

Rava said, "Be killed and do not kill; do you think that your blood is redder than his? Perhaps his blood is redder than yours."

(Talmud Pesachim 25b)

2. What does the following story from the Jerusalem Talmud teach regarding the saving of a life?

A group of people are walking along a road when they are stopped by heathens, who say to them, "Give us one of you and we will kill him. If not, we will kill all of you."

Let them all be killed, and let them not surrender one soul from Israel. But if the heathens single out one name, as with the case of Sheba ben Bichri, that person may be surrendered to them so that the others may be saved.

Rabbi Simeon ben Lakish said, "Only someone who is under a death sentence, the way Sheba ben Bichri was, may be turned over." But Rabbi Yochanan said, "Even someone who is not under sentence of death like Sheba ben Bichri" [but anyone whose name has been specified may be turned over].

(Jerusalem Talmud Terumot 8:10)

3. Lost in the Desert

The following is a story in the Talmud Baba Metzia 62a:

Two persons are lost in the desert. One of them has a water bottle. There is not enough water for two, so if they share it, both will surely die. If only one of them drinks the water, he or she may survive.

What should these people do? If you were in a similar situation, what would you do?

4. What is your opinion of Rabbi Ovadia Yosef, former Sephardic Chief Rabbi of Israel, who quotes the Jerusalem Talmud, stating, "If one stops to ask a rabbi whether it is permissible to desecrate the Sabbath and Yom Kippur in order to save a life, this delay is a form of murder."

5. What do you think Mishnah Sanhedrin 4:5 meant by, "Whoever saves one life, it is as if one saved the entire world"?

6. Deuteronomy commands us to "choose life, so that we may live" (*Deuteronomy 30:19*). What does this verse imply?

7. Not long ago Princess Diana was killed in a car crash in France. France has a "Good Samaritan" law which states that if one sees someone in danger and does not act, that person is guilty of a crime. How do you feel about such a law? How does the Good Samaritan law relate to the biblical law "you shall not stand by the blood of your neighbor" (*Leviticus 19:16*)?

8. What are some things that people can do every single day of their lives to save those whose lives are in danger?

GOOD MANNERS

דֶּרֶךְ אֶרֶץ

You should always be pleasant upon
entering and leaving a house.
(Leviticus 19:16)

What Does Judaism Have to Say?

The Code of Jewish Law is divided into four
sections, covering major aspects of Jewish behavior: ritual,
criminal and domestic. There is a fifth section which might
be called the laws of a human being, or in Hebrew, *hilchot
enoshut*. There is actually no complete single section on this
in the Code of Jewish Law, but rather we must rely on bits
and pieces of writings and sayings throughout the ages.

The Hebrew term *derech eretz* (literally, "the way of
the land") is difficult to define with precision. It has often
been understood as decency, decorum, proper etiquette,
good manners, common courtesy, and even *savoir faire*. But
the Hebrew term definitely has its ethical implications. As a
whole, *derech eretz* refers to a code of proper behavior
toward people.

Derech eretz is also the name of two lesser tractates
appended to the Babylonian Talmud. Derech Eretz
Rabbah, one of the tractates, emphasizes many rules by
using stories of the private lives of the sages. Derech Eretz
Zutah is a collection of ethical teachings consisting of a
variety of rules and correct behavior. It was originally
intended for scholars.

Rabbinic literature, in general, is replete with rules and suggestions on dignified conduct and common courtesy, covering almost every aspect of a person's conduct, including the most seemingly insignificant. Areas covered include proper speech, proper dress, the way to walk, how to eat and drink, treatment of other people and one's personal relations.

Derech eretz has been closely associated with the Torah itself. The rabbis have often commented that the two are inseparable, even claiming that *derech eretz* preceded the Torah. Here the probable meaning is that there are rules of conduct that are derived from common sense and are not explicitly spelled out in the Bible.

Jews are required to practice a code of acceptable behavior that goes beyond the formal observances. *Derech eretz,* though concerned primarily with a person's decent conduct toward fellow human beings, is unquestionably regarded as a religious obligation that God Himself requires.

Quotations on Good Manners

A. Communication

1. Never use an indecent expression, even if you have to use more words to complete the sentence.

(Talmud Pesachim 3a)

2. Accustom your tongue to say, "I do not know," lest you be led to falsehood and be apprehended.

(Derech Eretz Zutah, chap. 3)

3. A person should overlook an insult and not glorify himself by his fellow person's humiliation.

(Derech Eretz Zutah, chap. 6)

4. Keep aloof from making complaints, because if you complain against others you will be led to further sin.

(Derech Eretz Zutah, chap. 9)

5. Do not pacify your fellow in the hour of his anger, nor comfort him when his dead lies before him.

(Pirke Avot 4:23)

B. Teacher–Student

1. A student should visit his teacher every holiday.

(Talmud Rosh Hashanah 16b)

2. A person should never leave the company of his teacher or even his fellow unless he had previously obtained his consent.

(Derech Eretz Rabbah, chap. 5)

3. A scholar should not carry himself stiffly, with his neck outstretched, nor walk mincingly as do women and haughty people, nor run in a public place like a madman, nor bend his body as if he is a hunchback, but he should look downward, as when standing in prayer, and walk in the street like a person going about his business.

(Mishneh Torah Yad, De'ot 5:8)

C. Visiting and Being a Guest

1. The answer "yes" [to a knock on the door] does not mean "enter" but "wait."

(Talmud Baba Kamma 33a)

2. You should always be pleasant on entering and leaving a house.

(Derech Eretz Rabbah, chap. 4)

3. When two people sit at one table, the older of them puts forth his hand first (to pick up his portion from the dish), and then the younger. If the younger puts forth his hand first, he is deemed a glutton.

(Derech Eretz Rabbah, chap. 7)

4. A scholar should not eat standing, lick his fingers, or belch in the presence of his fellow.

(Derech Eretz Zutah, chap. 5)

5. No person should sit down at a table to eat before his elders have taken their seats.

(Derech Eretz Zutah, chap. 6)

D. Holidays and the Home

1. When a man gets angry in his house, he fixes his eyes upon the person of least importance.

(Mechilta,ii, 129)

E. Study of Torah Combined with Ethics

1. Rabbi Elazar ben Azariah said, "If there is no Torah, there is no *derech eretz*. And if there is no *derech eretz*, there is no Torah."

(Pirke Avot, 3:21)

2. Rabban Gamliel, the son of Rabbi Judah the Prince, said, "The study of Torah is good together with *derech eretz*, since the effort of both of them makes one forget sin.

(Pirke Avot, 2:2)

F. Miscellaneous

1. If you did someone a great favor, regard it as small, and do not say, "I did this good act with my own money." Rather, say it was from what God had graciously given you.

(Derech Eretz Zuta, 58a)

2. Concerning those who suffer insults but do not insult, who hear themselves reviled and do not answer back, who perform mitzvot from love and rejoice in their chastisement, the Bible declares, "But they that love God be as the sun when he goes forth in his might" *(Judges 5:31)*.

(Derech Eretz Rabbah 56a)

3. A person should not wear clothes of gold and purple, for instance, fit for a king and at which everyone stares, nor clothes worn by the poor that put to shame those wearing them, but he should wear modest dress.

(Mishneh Torah, Yad, De'ot 5:9)

4. Let all people learn good manners from the Omnipresent, Who stood at the entrance to Eden and called out to Adam, as it says, "The Lord called to Adam, saying, 'Where are you?'"

(Derech Eretz Rabbah 5)

Questions

1. What do you think the rabbis meant when they wrote in the *Pirke Avot*, "If there is no *derech eretz*, there is no Torah, and if there is no Torah, there is no *derech eretz*?

2. What are some common courtesies that you believe a student ought to afford his or her teacher? What is the *derech eretz* that you think teachers ought to extend to their students?

3. How often do you find yourself complimenting another person? Do you feel that you receive enough compliments in your daily life, or would you like to receive even more?

4. Have you ever had a teacher that you called by his or her first name? Why did you do so? Is it disrespectful (as the rabbis stated) to call a teacher by a first name?

5. Have you ever given up your seat on a bus or subway to an elderly person or a person who was obviously in need of a seat? How did it make you feel to do this?

6. "Running up the score" in sports means trying to score as many points as possible, even when you are already far ahead. College football teams sometimes run up the score. For instance, Florida State once clobbered Tulane by the score of 70–7. Some people believe that running up the score is bad sportsmanship. These people have argued that

football teams that are far ahead should send in their bench warmers and just try to run out the clock. Others argue that you play sports to win and it is insulting to the losing team if the winning team stops trying.

Do you believe that it is proper *derech eretz* to run up the score in a sporting event?

7. Here are some real-life occurrences. After reading each of them, decide what would be the courteous response (i.e. the *derech eretz* thing to do). See if you can find a connection between your decision and a rabbinic suggestion cited in the Quotations section.

You are a rabbi and read in your monthly rabbinical newsletter that one of your colleagues has recently published a new book.
Your response:
Rabbinic source:

You learn of the death of your friend's pet.
Your response:
Rabbinic source:

Your sister or brother buys a new sweater and offers you a fashion show, but you are doing something else at the time.
Your response:
Rabbinic source:

D. You are shopping for clothing in a large department store and the salesperson is extremely courteous and helpful to you.
Your response:
Rabbinic source:

You call someone on the phone and when she answers you realize that you have reached the wrong number.
Your response:
Rabbinic source:

As class representative, you receive a phone call from an angry classmate who begins to scream, rant and rave.
Your response:
Rabbinic source:

8. Truth Combined with Derech Eretz

Following is a famous talmudic story from tractate Ketubot 16b–17a. After reading the story, answer the questions that follow:

An argument began between the two famous rabbinic schools of Hillel and Shammai. Their argument relates to whether or not a person ought to compliment a bride even if, in the eyes of the perceiver, she is not particularly good looking. The story goes like this:
Our rabbis taught: "How does one dance before the bride?"
Bet Shammai says: "A bride as she is."
But Bet Hillel says: "A beautiful and graceful bride."
Bet Shammai said to Bet Hillel: "If she were lame or blind, would you say to her 'a beautiful and graceful bride,' since the Torah says, 'Keep far from falsehood' [*Exodus 23:7*]?
Bet Hillel said to Bet Shammai: "According to you, one who made a bad purchase in the market, should you praise it before him or defame it? Surely you should praise it. Therefore, the sages concluded, 'One should always be pleasant toward people.'"

How does this story relate to the concept of *derech eretz*? Do you agree with the conclusion of the rabbis? Would you compliment a person regardless of whether or not that person truly deserved the compliment?

9. *Mensch* is a term often used to refer to the kind of person God had in mind when God arranged for human creation. A *mensch* is someone who is humble, reliable, honest, dependable, unselfish, kind, and always sensitive to the feelings of others. Here are some more real-life situations. In each case, the person is one who strives to live his or her life according to the laws of *derech eretz*. In each situation, what should this person do?

1. A person has invited some friends over to his home for dinner. The meal has just begun when one of his friends spills some of his beverage on the floor.

2. A young person is riding on her school bus as a new school year begins. For several days in a row she encounters several of her classmates on the bus teasing a new child on the block.

3. A basketball coach is playing a lopsided game, with his team winning by a huge margin. The other team seems to be totally embarrassed by its performance.

4. A girl and her best friend have competed for the top science award in the class. The day of reckoning arrives, and the girl receives a phone call from the science staff that she has been declared the winner.

10. The prophet Micah provided advice as to what God wants of people: "Do justly, love goodness, and walk humbly with God" (*6:8*).

What is your advice regarding what you think God truly wants of people?

Univ. City

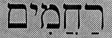

COMPASSION

רַחֲמִים

You shall not wrong a stranger or oppress him,
for you were strangers in the land of Egypt.
(Exodus 22:20)

What Does Judaism Have to Say?

The Torah has always understood how much a part of human nature it is to take advantage of society's weakest people. Such marginal members of society might include the elderly, the bereaved, those seeking political asylum in a new land, the poor, the weak, the widow and orphan, the homeless, people with physical disabilities such as the sight and hearing impaired, and the sick. Thus the Torah is filled with commandments related to helping these people. For instance, concerning the stranger it states: "You shall not wrong a stranger or oppress him, for you were strangers in the land of Egypt. You shall not ill-treat any widow or orphan" *(Exodus 22:20–21)*. Concerning strangers, the Torah claims that they are the sole category of people whom God is identified as loving. The Bible says: "And God loves the stranger."

A traditional prayer appearing in the Passover Haggadah recited near the beginning of the Passover seder states, "Let all who are hungry come in and eat; let all who are needy come in and make Passover."

There are in rabbinic literature a variety of statements and laws related to visiting and helping the sick. Visiting-the-sick societies, known as *bikkur cholim* groups, were prevalent in many European Jewish communities. During the last century Jewish immigrants to North America also helped to establish such societies, which have continued in many communities to this day. In some congregations and communities, *bikkur cholim* societies have been replaced by caring committees which do essentially the same mitzvah and more. The vocabulary may have changed, but the mitzvah work remains the same: caring and comforting those who are ill.

Caring for the dead and the bereaved is another important religious obligation. The Hebrew phrase *chesed shel emet* (true act of kindness) is used to refer to caring for the dead and the bereaved, since no one can accuse the individual of doing this kind of mitzvah for personal gain. As a result, this act of kindness, and everything that goes with it, is highly praised in Jewish tradition. Many communities today have what are called the *chevra kaddisha* (holy burial society), consisting of volunteers from the community who not only help prepare the deceased for burial but assist the bereaved family in making funeral arrangements and the like. The pain of losing someone we love can be all-consuming, robbing the individual of the ability to think clearly for a period of time. The work of the *chevra kaddisha* becomes all the more important when bereavement strikes.

Quotations on Compassion

1. You shall not wrong a stranger or oppress him, for you were strangers in the land of Egypt. You shall not mistreat any widow or orphan.

(Exodus 22:20–21)

2. A person must be heedful of his behavior toward widows and orphans, because their souls are deeply depressed and their spirits low. Even if they are wealthy, even if they are the widow and orphans of a king, we are warned concerning them, "You shall not ill-treat any widow or orphan." How are we to conduct ourselves toward them?

One must always speak to them tenderly. One must show them unwavering courtesy, not hurt them physically with hard toil, or wound their feelings with harsh speech. One must take greater care of their property and money than of one's own. Whoever irritates them, provokes them to anger, pains them, tyrannizes them, or causes them loss of money, is guilty of a transgression.

*(Mishneh Torah, Laws of Character
Development and Ethical Conduct 6:10)*

3. You shall not place a stumbling block in front of a blind person: You shall fear God.

(Leviticus 19:14)

4. If a man seeks your advice, do not give him counsel that is wrong for him. Do not say to him, "Leave early in the morning," so that thugs might mug him.

(Sifra Leviticus on 19:14)

5. It happened that one of Rabbi Akiva's students became sick, but none of the sages went to visit him. Rabbi Akiva, however, went to visit him. Because he swept and cleaned the floor for him, the student recovered. The student said to him, "Rabbi, you have given me life." Rabbi Akiva came out and taught, "Those who do not visit a sick person might just as well have spilled his blood."

(Talmud Nedarim 40a)

6. You shall not return a runaway slave to his master. Let him stay with you anywhere he chooses in any one of your settlements, whatever suits him best. You shall not wrong him.

(Deuteronomy 23:16–17)

7. To minister to the sick is to minister to God.

(Abraham Joshua Heschel)

8. The rabbis taught that visiting the sick is one of the mitzvot for which a person enjoys the fruits in this world, but the real reward is held for the individual in what the rabbis described as the World to Come.

(Talmud Shabbat 127a)

9. Rescue those who are drawn to death.

(Proverbs 24:11)

10. Do not harden your heart or shut your hand against your needy kinsman.

(Deuteronomy 15:7)

Questions

1. Redeeming or saving captives, according to Moses Maimonides, takes precedence over supporting the poor or clothing them. Suppose a building was on fire and within the building there were people of many different ages and professions. Among them were teachers, scholars, lawyers, doctors, and children of various ages. What characteristics or circumstances should be taken into account when deciding whom to try to save first?

2. What kinds of people or families in your own community are most in need of help? What are you or your community doing to assist them?

3. When you are sick, how is your state of mind? What kinds of things make you feel better or help you to recover more quickly?

4. What are some of the advantages of people from a particular congregation visiting fellow congregants in the hospital, even those they do not know well?

5. Why do you think the rabbis regarded preparing a human body for burial as a sincere act of kindness?

6. In general, what can the synagogue community do to help mourners during the *shiva* period and afterwards, after the individual moves into the periods of less intense mourning.

7. Leviticus 19:14 states, "Do not place a stumbling block before a blind person." What does this verse mean? To what kind of stumbling blocks might the Bible refer?

8. What did Abraham Joshua Heschel mean when he said, "To minister to the sick is to minister to God"?

9. The Bible often speaks of the triad of "widows, orphans, and strangers." What do widows, orphans, and strangers have in common? What are their common special needs?

10. The philosopher Hermann Cohen once wrote that the biblical commandments protecting the stranger represented the beginning of true religion. Do you agree with this statement? If not, what do you think represents the beginning of "true religion"?

HONORING THE DEAD AND
COMFORTING MOURNERS

חֶסֶד שֶׁל אֱמֶת

Weeping may linger at night,
but joy comes with the dawn.
(Psalm 30:6)

What Does Judaism Have to Say?

Chesed shel emet means a true act of kindness. It is used in Jewish tradition to refer to caring for the dead, since no one can accuse an individual of doing this mitzvah for personal gain. After all, the person who is being served by the mitzvah is dead. Therefore, this supreme act of kindness, and everything that goes along with it, is highly praised in Judaism.

Our society is a death-denying one. People do not want to talk about death. Some are uncomfortable with the idea of preparing a human body for burial. Such discussions may remind us of our own mortality, the reality that we too will die one day. Nevertheless, in Judaism the preparation and burial of the human body, along with comforting the bereaved, has traditionally held a place near the top of the ladder of doing mitzvot.

Arranging for the burial of a corpse that is lying unattended is a religious duty (called *met mitzvah*.) The duty of burying it devolves upon any person who discovers it. The term *met mitzvah*, strictly speaking, applies to the dead body of a person whose relatives are unknown. The burial is obligatory on everybody. In the days of the Temple, even a high priest was expected to perform the last offices for the unburied dead. The unwritten law about the burial of the neglected dead was regarded as a duty of the highest obligation in ancient Israel, as it is in the talmudic law.

In the book of Tobit in the Apocrypha we read: "If I saw one of my people dead and thrown outside the wall of Nineveh, I would bury him. I buried them secretly, for he killed many in his anger. My neighbors laughed at me and said 'here he is burying the dead again.'" (1:17–18; 2:4–8). By extension, *met mitzvah* is the equivalent of *halvayat hamet,* which means accompanying the dead to their last resting place.

One of the early references to burial is found in the Book of Deuteronomy. There we learn that "a person must not let a human body remain on the stake overnight but must bury it the same day" (Deuteronomy 21:23). From this biblical verse the rabbis deduced that it is preferable to bury a dead person within 24 hours, unless there are circumstances that prevent doing so. Things that might legitimately delay burial include waiting for out-of-town relatives to arrive. Thus we have an obligation to care for the dead and also comfort the living.

There is hardly a Jewish community in the world without a *chevra kaddisha*—a holy burial society—which watches over the dead person and helps prepare it for burial in a ritual called the *tahara* (ritual purification). The *chevra kaddisha,* a volunteer organization, is charged with washing the body, reciting psalms in honor of the deceased, and dressing the body in a shroud, a simple garment made of white linen or cotton (symbolizing purity). In the past, cemeteries had their own rooms for performing the ritual of purification; today the washing of the body usually takes place at the funeral home.

Friends of the deceased are often asked to carry the casket to the grave as pallbearers. In addition, it is becoming customary for both friends and relatives of the deceased to deliver the eulogy at the funeral service. Expressing words of comfort to the bereaved and words of honor in memory of the departed is another act of true kindness which is selfless and can never be repaid.

In the Book of Job we are told that when Job's friends learned of his misfortune, they came together to give him sympathy and comfort: "They sat upon the ground with him for seven days and seven nights, but none of them spoke a word to him, for they saw how great was his suffering" (Job 2:11–13). Today, it is customary, after the burial, for the mourners to return to the home of the deceased to sit shiva. *Shiva,* from the Hebrew word for "seven," refers to the first seven days of mourning. During this period the immediate family stays together, in this way receiving the mutual support and comfort necessary to face the challenge of their loss. During shiva, friends and community members, as well as other family members, visit to express their sympathy. In order for the mourners to focus on their loss, but also because friends are concerned that the mourners eat properly, the first meal following the funeral, known as the meal of condolence, is provided by friends. This is another way that friends extend themselves to mourners. Most of the time, there is nothing that can actually be said to soften the pain. Just being there and reaching out to people can help them with the pain they feel.

Questions on Honoring the Dead and Comforting Mourners

1. Rabbi Yochanan said: "Comforters are not allowed to say a word until the mourner begins the conversation."

(Talmud Moed Katan 28b)

2. Silence is meritorious in a house of mourning.

(Talmud Berachot 6b)

3. Even as the deceased are requited, so are the eulogizers who are untruthful and they who echo the falsehoods spoken by them.

(Talmud Berachot 62a)

4. When a person sheds tears at the death of a virtuous person, the Holy One counts them and places them in His treasure house."

(Talmud Shabbat 105a)

5. Those who are standing in the presence of the dead at a funeral are not standing in honor of the deceased, but in honor of those who are performing an act of kindness for the deceased."

(Jerusalem Talmud Bikkurim 3:3)

Questions

1. Why do you think the rabbis regarded preparing a human body for burial as one of the highest forms of kindness? Can you think of other things one might do for someone else that you would consider a supreme act of kindness?

2. The pain of losing someone we love can be all-consuming, robbing a person of the ability to think clearly for a period of time. Some people believe that a burial society, since it is voluntary and nonprofit, prevents unscrupulous individuals from taking advantage of mourners during this time of intense pain. What are some abuses that might occur in communities with no burial society?

3. Do some research and look into what your own community does for mourners during shiva.

4. If your community has a *chevra kaddisha*, contact one of its members and interview him or her about the activities of the society.

5. In the Talmud, Rabbi Yochanan teaches us that "comforters are not permitted to say a word until the mourner begins the conversation." What do you think motivated Rabbi Yochanan to make that suggestion? Do you agree with his advice? What advice of your own would you give to someone who was about to pay a shiva call?

6. The traditional words of comfort to a mourner are: *Hamakom y'nachem etchem betoch she'ar avaylay tziyon veyerushalayim*, "may God comfort you among the mourners for Zion and Jerusalem." Why do you think the rabbis added the phrase "among the mourners for Zion and Jerusalem"? What purpose does this additional phrase serve?

7. Traditional Judaism requires that a person who has died be buried within 24 hours. What do you think is the reasoning behind this law? Do some research and see what Roman Catholicism requires after a person has died. Compare and contrast its ways with the Jewish way.

8. Many traditional communities arrange for a *shomer* (watchperson) to be at the side of the deceased at all times. This person, or several persons taking turns, often recites psalms and meditates through the "watch." What is your opinion of this custom? What do you think is the rationale behind it?

9. Unlike in many other religions, traditional Jewish law requires that mourners and friends cover the coffin with spadefuls of dirt, a difficult task indeed for any person. What function do you think this tradition serves?

10. Research the reasons why Jewish law frowns upon cremation.

For Further Reading

Chavel, Charles E. *Between Man and His Fellow Man*. New York: Shiloh, 1980.

Finkel, Abraham Yaakov, trans. *Sefer Chasidim: The Book of the Pious*. Northvale, NJ: Jason Aronson, 1997.

Isaacs, Ron. *Derech Eretz: The Path to an Ethical Life*. New York: United Synagogue of Conservative Judaism Department of Youth Activities, 1995.

Kurshan, Neil. *Raising Your Child to Be a Mensch*. New York: Atheneum, 1987.

Rittner, Stephen. *Jewish Ethics for the 21st Century*. MA: Stephen Rittner, 1977.

Summers, Barbara Fortgang. *Community and Responsibility in the Jewish Tradition*. New York: United Synagogue of Conservative Judaism Department of Youth Activities, 1978.

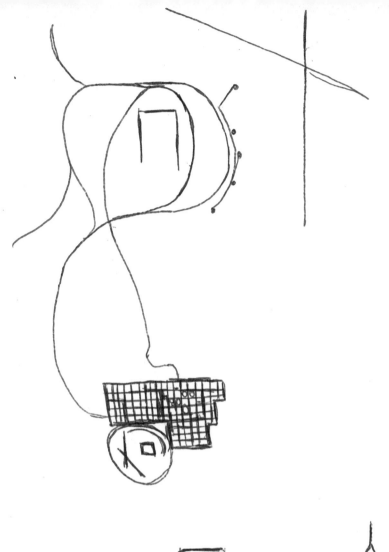

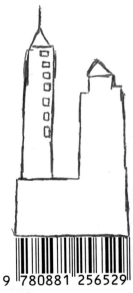

Printed in the United States
204434BV00001B/190-219/A